PREPARE,

PRESENT

AND

PRACTICE

THE DETAILS OF A KODALY BASED PROGRAM

BY
MAXINE BEASLEY

authorHOUSE™

1663 LIBERTY DRIVE, SUITE 200
BLOOMINGTON, INDIANA 47403
(800) 839-8640
WWW.AUTHORHOUSE.COM

First published by AuthorHouse 04/13/05

ISBN: 1-4208-2864-9 (sc)

Printed in the United States of America
Bloomington, Indiana

This book is printed on acid-free paper.

NOTES FROM THE AUTHOR

Upon completion of a Kodaly certification program, the need for plans to develop a method of PREPARING, PRESENTING and PRACTICING a concept was still a challenge. The following lessons were developed as a means to provide a solution to the problem. Consideration had to be given to teacher grade assignment and previous music study by students.

The plans were taught to fourth and fifth grade students at Ogden Elementary school in Beaumont, Texas. These students had no previous knowledge of the Kodaly method. Classes were held twice a week for forty-five minutes. Success of the program was apparent by the students participation in Middle and High school music organizations.

SUGGESTIONS FOR USE;
1. As they are written.
2. As a guide to extend concept.
3. Work sheets may be copied for class use.
4. Lessons may be copied and turned in to Principal.
5. Song materials attached may be copied and placed in binders for class use.

TEACHER NEEDS KNOWLEDGE OF;
1. How to teach a song using the rote method.
2. Some effective inner hearing exercises.
3. Simple part work.
4. Songs suitable for use in a certain concept.
5. A sponge activity.

SUGGESTION FOR IDENTIFYING AN UNKNOWN PITCH;
1. Class sings words of the song then sings the rhythm.
2. Rhythm is written on board.
3. Teacher draws tone ladder on board. Labels known steps. Places an X in a circle on side of the tone ladder.
4. Teacher sings song with pitch syllables. Points to the steps on the tone ladder. Points to the X and hums when that tone is sung.
5. Class repeats step 4 while the teacher points to the steps and to the X.
6. This is repeated several times. The pitch letters are then written under the rhythm including the X on the tones where it occurs.
7. Class is lead into a discussion about the new tone. Such questions as is it higher or lower than another specified tone etc.
8. Students are lead to name the tone, given the hand sign, and places it on the tone ladder.
9. Class sings song again using the new pitch name. Then sings again using pitch names and hand signs.

TABLE OF CONTENTS

RHYTHM SYLLABLES

STEM NOTATION   **NOTE**

ta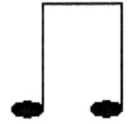

titi

rest

too-oo

tiritiri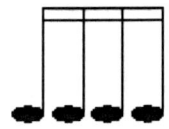

ti tiri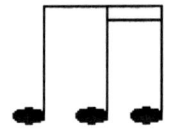

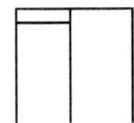 tiri ti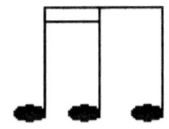

too-oo-ee

syn co pa

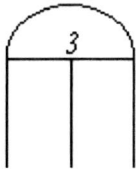 too-oo-ee-oo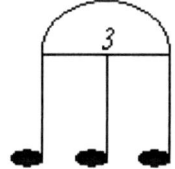

ti tum

3   3

triola

teem ri

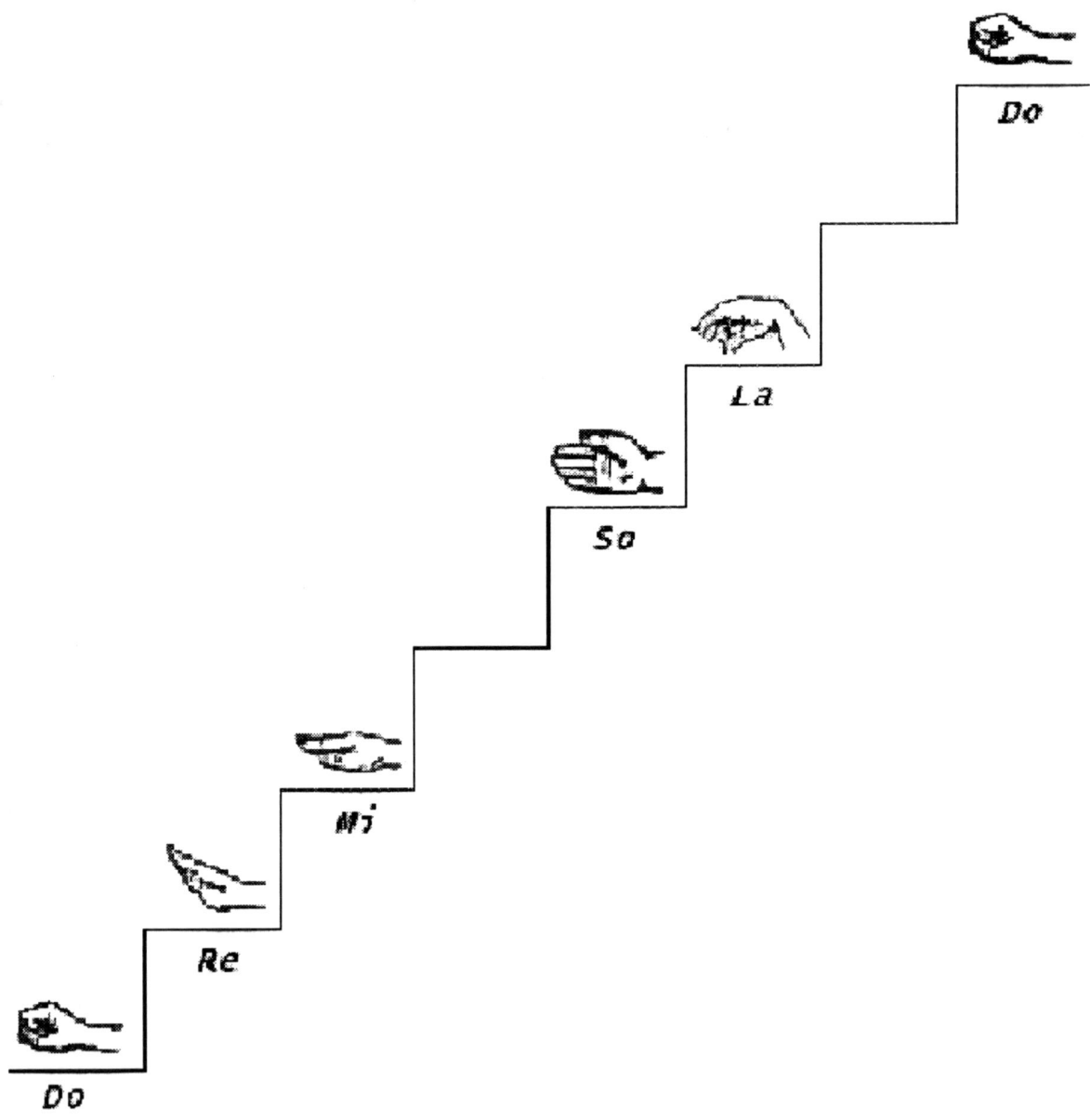

Do

Re

Mi

So

La

Do

RHYTHM MANIPULATIVES

MATERIALS;
1. 25 quart size plastic bags. (7in. x 8in.)
2. Laminated poster boards. Any color and as many as needed to make rhythm signs for 25 packages.
3. Scissors.

PROCEDURE;
1. Run a copy of the rhythm signs.
2. Cut out signs and use as patterns for poster board cut out.
3. Numbers over rhythm signs indicate how many to place in each package.
4. Each package should contain seven or eight rhythm signs.

1

3

1 or 2

1

1

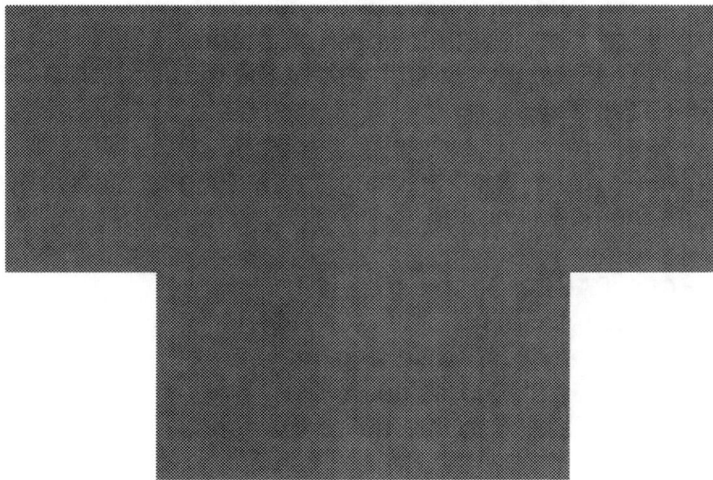

LESSON 1

INSTRUCTIONAL OBJECTIVES;
1. PREPARE (a) so mi. (b) the beat.
2. PRESENT definitions for; music, pitch, beat, and dynamics.

BEHAVIORAL OBJECTIVES; students will;
1. Learn a song. (INSTRUCTIONAL OBJECTIVE 1)
2. Learn a rhyme. (INSTRUCTIONAL OBJECTIVE 2)
3. Learn definitions and apply these definitions. (INSTRUCTIONAL OBJECTIVE 3)

MATERIALS; 1. SONG; "RAIN RAIN." 2. RHYME; "QUEEN, QUEEN." 3. MAGNETIC BOARD, MAGNETIC WORDS FOR "QUEEN, QUEEN," AND MAGNETIC HEARTS. 4. SOMETHING TO HIDE WHILE PLAYING THE DYNAMICS GAME.

PROCEDURE;
1. Prepare seating plan.
2. Instruction is given on class rules and school rules.
3. Instruction is given on how to sing the greeting.

| (Teacher) | Hel - | | child- | | (class) | Hel - | | teach- |
| | | lo | | dren. | | | lo | | er. |

STATE OBJECTIVES;

4. Teacher defines the following terms:
    a. MUSIC;   The art of sound in time.
    b. BEAT;   The repeated pulse of the music.
    c. PITCH;   The highness or lowness of a tone.
    d. DYNAMICS;   The loudness or softness of the music.
(BEHAVIORAL OBJECTIVE 3)

5. Teacher then gives instruction on learning a new song or a new rhyme by rote. Teacher presents the new song.

6. NEW SONG; "RAIN, RAIN." On this they will;
    a. Learn the song by rote (PITCH APPLICATION)
    b. Learn to keep a steady beat while singing.
    c. Learn to clap the way the words go.
    d. Learn to use inner hearing to internalize the song.
(BEHAVIORAL OBJECTIVE 1)

7. NEW RHYME; "Queen, Queen." On this they will;
   a. Learn the rhyme by rote.
   b. Learn to clap the beat. (tap desk, clap hands)
   c. Keep the beat and say the rhyme.
   d. Class observes as teacher places words on the magnetic board and demonstrates how to find words that come with a beat. A heart is placed under words that come with a beat.
   e. Class says the rhyme and claps the beat. This time paying special attention to words that come with a beat.
(BEHAVIORAL OBJECTIVE 2)

8. PRESENT DYNAMICS; Teacher explains that the music can be soft or loud. Class is instructed to give 4 loud claps followed by 4 soft claps. Do this until the teacher says stop. Other patterns of loud/soft claps may be given. For example 2 loud claps and 2 soft claps. This activity is followed by playing the dynamics game.

   DYNAMICS GAME: The teacher or a student hides an object, a book, a handkerchief etc. One child is sent out of the room. The object is hidden. When the child returns, he or she must find the hidden object. If he or she gets close to the object the class claps loud. When the student is not close to the object, the class claps soft. The clapping never stops, just changes from loud to soft. When the object is found then the game starts over. (DYNAMICS APPLICATION)

9. CLOSURE: 1. Name the song learned today. 2. Name the rhyme learned today. 3. Review terms learned today.

10. GOOD-BYE: Teacher demonstrates ow to sing the good-bye.
    (teacher)   Good -   child-   (class)   Good -   teach-
                  bye   dren.   bye   er.

RAIN, RAIN GO AWAY

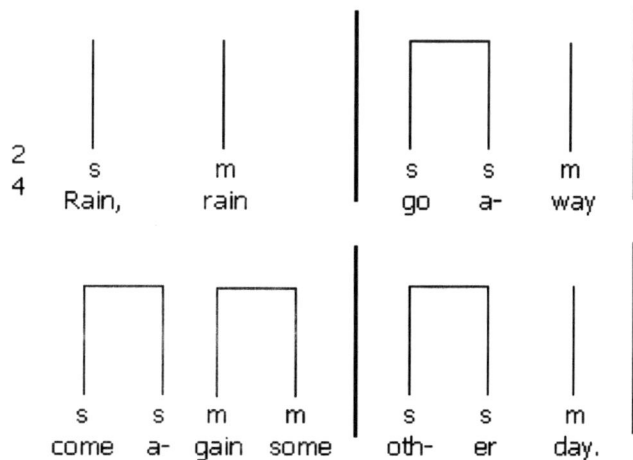

2

QUEEN, QUEEN CAROLINE

Queen,   Queen   Ca-   ro-   line.

Washed her   hair   in   tur-   pen-   tine.

Tur-   pen-   tine   made   it   shine.

Queen,   Queen   Ca-   ro-   line.

LESSON 2
INSTRUCTIONAL OBJECTIVES;
1. PREPARE (a) so mi. (b) the beat.
2. PRESENT writing the beat.
3. PRACTICE clapping the beat and saying a familiar rhyme.

BEHAVIORAL OBJECTIVES; students will;
1. Learn a new song. (INSTRUCTIONAL OBJECTIVE 1)
2. Learn a new rhyme. (INSTRUCTIONAL OBJECTIVE 2)
3. Place beats under the words of a familiar rhyme. (INSTRUCTIONAL OBJECTIVE 3)
4. Clap the beat and say the words to "Queen, Queen." (INSTRUCTIONAL OBJECTIVE 4)

MATERIALS; 1. SONG; "QUAKER, QUAKER." 2. RHYME; "ENGINE, ENGINE."
3. MAGNETIC BOARD, MAGNETIC WORDS FOR "QUEEN, QUEEN," AND MAGNETIC
HEARTS.

PROCEDURE;
1. GREETING; sung as Hel -   child-   (class)   Hel -   teach-
                                         lo   dren.   lo   er.
2. OPENING SONG; "Rain, Rain." On this they will;
   a. Sing the words and clap the beat.
   b. Do some form of part work.

STATE OBJECTIVES;

3. NEW SONG; "Quaker, Quaker." On this they will;
   a. Learn the song by rote.
   b. Clap the beat and say the words.
   c. Clap the way the words go.
   d. Use inner hearing to internalize the song.
(BEHAVIORAL OBJECTIVE 1)

4. NEW RHYME; "Engine, Engine." On this they will;
   a. Learn the rhyme by rote.
   b. Clap the beat and say the words.
   c. Clap the way the words go.
   d. Use inner hearing to internalize the rhyme.
(BEHAVIORAL OBJECTIVE 2)

5. PRESENT WRITING THE BEAT; Presentation rhyme "Queen, Queen."
   Method of presentation.
   a. Define beat as the repeated pulse of the music.
   b. Class recites the rhyme and keeps the beat.
   c. Teacher places the words for the rhyme on the magnetic board.
   d. Each student is given a heart to place under a word that comes with a beat. The
      work is checked and corrections are made.
   (THIS IS A PICTURE OF THE REPEATED PULSE OF THE BEAT)
(BEHAVIORAL OBJECTIVE 3)

6. STUDENT PERFORMANCE; Students come before the class in a group and play the beat on sticks while saying the words to "Queen, Queen."
(BEHAVIORAL OBJECTIVE 4)

7. CLOSURE; 1. Name the new song learned today. 2. Name the new rhyme learned today. 3. Define beat.

8. GOOD-BYE; sung as; Good-   child-   (class) Good-   teach-
                            bye   dren.   bye   er.

WRITE ON BOARD; 1. LEARN A NEW SONG. 2. LEARN A NEW RHYME. 3. LEARN TO WRITE THE BEAT. 4. PLAY THE BEAT WHILE SAYING THE RHYME.

QUAKER, QUAKER

Group 1 (Question)

4
4 Quak- er,   Qua- ker   how is   thee?

s   s   m   m   s   s   m

How's thy neigh- bor next to thee?

s   s   m   m   s   s   m

Group 2 (Answer)

Ve- ry   well   I   thank thee.

s   s   m   s   s   m

I   don't know I'll   go   and   see.

s   s   m   m   s   s   m

ENGINE, ENGINE

En- gine,   en- gine num- ber   nine.

Go- ing   down Chi- ca- go   line.

If   the   train goes off the   track.

Do   you   want your mon- ey   back?

LESSON 3
INSTRUCTIONAL OBJECTIVES;
1. PRESENT rhythm.
2. PRACTICE identifying long and short sounds.

BEHAVIORAL OBJECTIVES; students will;
1. Learn a new rhyme. (INSTRUCTIONAL OBJECTIVE 1)
2. Learn the definition of rhythm. (INSTRUCTIONAL OBJECTIVE 2)
3. Visually and aurally identify long and short sounds. (INSTRUCTIONAL OBJECTIVE 3)

MATERIALS; 1. RHYME; "2, 4, 6, 8." 2. TEACHER SELECTED RHYTHM LISTENING
MATERIAL. 3. MAGNETIC BOARD, MAGNETIC WORDS FOR "ENGINE, ENGINE" AND
MAGNETIC LONG AND SHORT STRIPS.

PROCEDURE;
1. GREETING; sung as Hel -   child-   (class)   Hel -   teach-
                        lo   dren.   lo   er.

2. OPENING SONG; "QUAKER, QUAKER." On this they will;
    a. Sing the words and clap the beat.
    b. Do some form of part work.

STATE OBJECTIVES;

3. NEW RHYME; "2, 4, 6, 8." On this they will;
    a. Learn the rhyme by rote.
    b. Clap the beat and say the words.
    c. Clap the way the words go.
    d. Use inner hearing to internalize the rhyme.
(BEHAVIORAL OBJECTIVE 1)

A NOTE TO THE TEACHER: YOU MAY CHOOSE ACTIVITY 5 OR 6. HOWEVER, BOTH
ACTIVITIES MAY BE USED.

4. PRESENT RHYTHM; method of presentation;
    a. Define rhythm as long and short sounds.
    b. Class recites "Engine, Engine."
    c. Teacher places the words on the magnetic board, four lines with four beats on
       each line.
    d. Teacher claps the way the words go while saying the words.
    e. Class does the same.
    f. Teacher demonstrates how to place strips under the words showing a long or short
       sound.
    g. Strips are removed and class is given an opportunity to do the same. (THIS IS A
       PICTURE OF LONG AND SHORT SOUNDS)

5. LISTENING ACTIVITY; suggested materials;
    a. Sesame Street Long and Short Sounds.
    b. State adopted text section on rhythm.
(BEHAVIORAL OBJECTIVES 2 AND 3)

6. STUDENT PERFORMANCE; Divide the class into two groups. One group claps the beat while the other group claps the words of a familiar song or rhyme. Exchange parts.

7. CLOSURE; 1. Name the new rhyme learned today. 2. Define rhythm. 3. Define beat.

8. GOOD-BYE; sung as; Good-   child-   (class) Good-   teach-
                          bye   dren.   bye   er.

WRITE ON BOARD; 1. LEARN A NEW RHYME. 2. LEARN ABOUT RHYTHM. 3. PERFORM RHYTHM AND BEAT.

TWO, FOUR, SIX, EIGHT

| | | |

Two   four   six   eight.

Meet me   at   the   gar- den gate.

If   I'm   late   don't   wait.

Two   four   six   eight.

LESSON 4
INSTRUCTIONAL OBJECTIVES;
1. PREPARE ta and titi.
2. PRESENT pitch, melody and contour.
3. PRACTICE writing contour.

BEHAVIORAL OBJECTIVES; students will;
1. Learn a new rhyme. (INSTRUCTIONAL OBJECTIVE 1)
2. Learn the definitions for pitch, melody, and contour. (INSTRUCTIONAL OBJECTIVE 2)
3. Write the words of a familiar song in contour. (INSTRUCTIONAL OBJECTIVE 3)

MATERIALS; 1. RHYME; "BEE, BEE BUMBLE BEE." 2. SMALL FLANNEL BOARDS AND FELT
CIRCLES. LARGE FLANNEL BOARD FOR TEACHER. 3. MAGNETIC BOARD, MAGNETIC
WORDS FOR "RAIN, RAIN."

PROCEDURE;
1. GREETING; sung as Hel-   child-   (class)   Hel-   teach-
                           lo   dren.   lo   er.
2. OPENING; Familiar songs and rhymes. On these they will;
   a. Sing or say the words and clap the beat.
   b. Do some form of part work.

STATE OBJECTIVES;

3. NEW RHYME; "Bee, Bee Bumble Bee." On this they will;
   a. Learn the rhyme by rote.
   b. Clap the beat and say the words.
   c. Clap the way the words go.
   d. Use inner hearing to internalize the rhyme.
(BEHAVIORAL OBJECTIVE 1)

4. PRESENT PITCH, MELODY, AND CONTOUR; method of presentation;
   a. Define each term.
   b. Distribute flannel boards and four felt circles. Rules are given for using these
      materials.
   c. Teacher models what is to be done. Students are instructed to place the four
      circles in a high, low, or repeated pattern according to what they hear sung on a
      loo.
      1. Teacher sings the pattern on a loo;
         loo   loo
             loo   loo
      2. Students sing answer as;
         high   high
             low   low
      3. Students place felt circles on flannel board showing the contour of the pattern.
      4. Teacher places circles on big flannel board so students can check their
         answers.
(BEHAVIORAL OBJECTIVE 2)

9

5. WRITING ACTIVITY; Teacher with class assistance will write the words of a familiar song in contour on the magnetic board.
   a. Teacher places word to "Rain, Rain" on the magnetic board in a straight line.
   b. Teacher sings the words as they look on one tone.
      (q) Is this the tune of this song? (ans.) no.
   c. Teacher: "I will sing the song again and you will tell me if the word is to be moved high, low, or remain in the same place."
   d. After the song has been written in contour, the class sings the song again this time observing the high, low, or repeated tones.
   e. Students are given an opportunity to write the words in contour. Other familiar songs may be used also.

(BEHAVIORAL OBJECTIVE 3)

1. CLOSURE; 1. Name the new rhyme learned today. 2. Define pitch. 3. Define melody. 4. Define contour.

2. GOOD-BYE; sung as; Good-   child-   (class) Good-   teach-
                         bye   dren.   bye   er.

WRITE ON BOARD; 1. LEARN A NEW RHYME. 2. LEARN ABOUT PITCH. 3. LEARN ABOUT MELODY. 4. LEARN ABOUT CONTOUR.

BEE, BEE BUMBLE BEE

| | | | |
Bee,   bee,   bum- ble-   bee.

Stung a   man up-   on his   knee.

Stung a   pig up-   on his   snout.

I   de-   clare that   you are   out!

LESSON 4 GRADE _____ TEACHER_____

LESSON 5
INSTRUCTIONAL OBJECTIVES;
1. PREPARE the quarter rest.
2. PRESENT dynamics.
3. PRACTICE dynamics.

BEHAVIORAL OBJECTIVES; students will;
1. Learn a new song. (INSTRUCTIONAL OBJECTIVE 1)
2. Learn about dynamics. (INSTRUCTIONAL OBJECTIVE 2)
3. Aurally identify loud and soft in a musical selection. (INSTRUCTIONAL OBJECTIVE 3)

MATERIALS; 1. SONG; "IN AND OUT." 2. ON MAGNETIC BOARD, THE WORD DYNAMICS, THE WORD LOUD, THE WORD SOFT, THE WORD FORTE, THE WORD PIANO, ALL THE LETTERS USED TO IDENTIFY LOUD AND SOFT. 3. TEACHER SELECTED DYNAMICS LISTENING MATERIAL AND WORKSHEET. 4. PENCILS. 5. STICKS.

PROCEDURE;
1. GREETING; sung as Hel -   child-   (class)   Hel -   teach-
                    lo   dren.   lo   er.

2. OPENING; Familiar songs and rhymes. On these they will;
   a. Sing the words and clap the beat.
   b. Do some form of part work.

STATE OBJECTIVES;

3. NEW SONG; "In and Out." On this they will;
   a. Learn the song by rote.
   b. Clap the beat and sing the words.
   c. Clap the way the words go.
   d. Sing the words and show the pitch by raising or lowering the hands.
   e. Use inner hearing to internalize the song.
(BEHAVIORAL OBJECTIVE 1)

4. PRESENT DYNAMICS; method of presentation;
   a. Define dynamics.
   b. Teacher explains that the music can be loud or soft. There are symbols to tell when the music is soft or when it is loud. Teacher places the word dynamics at the top of the magnetic board. The words soft and piano are placed on the left side, and the words loud and forte are placed on the right side. Teacher explains the words piano and forte in relationship to dynamics. All symbols meaning loud are placed under the word loud. Emphasize; Any symbol with a p is the soft family. Any symbol with an f is in the loud family.
(BEHAVIORAL OBJECTIVE 2)

5. LISTENING ACTIVITY; Teacher chooses method of presentation.
(BEHAVIORAL OBJECTIVE 3)

6. STUDENT PERFORMANCE; Students will play the beat on sticks while singing a familiar song or saying a familiar rhyme. On this they will perform a dynamics according to the dynamic sign held up by the teacher or student.

7. CLOSURE; 1. Name the new song learned today. 2. Define dynamics.

8. GOOD-BYE; sung as; Good-   child-   (class) Good-   teach-
                            bye   dren.   bye   er.

WRITE ON BOARD; 1. LEARN A NEW SONG. 2. LEARN ABOUT DYNAMICS.

IN AND OUT

| 4 | s | m | s | _ | s | m | s | _ |
| 4 | In | and | out | | round | a- | bout | |

| s | m | s | m | s | m | s | _ |
| O | U | T | and | that | spells | out. | |

LESSON 5 GRADE_____ TEACHER_____

LESSON 6

INSTRUCTIONAL OBJECTIVES;
1. PREPARE so mi.
2. PRESENT tempo.
3. PRACTICE tempo.

BEHAVIORAL OBJECTIVES; students will;
1. Learn a new song. (INSTRUCTIONAL OBJECTIVE 1)
2. Learn about tempo. (INSTRUCTIONAL OBJECTIVE 2)
3. Aurally identify tempo in a musical selection. (INSTRUCTIONAL OBJECTIVE 3)

MATERIALS; 1. SONG; "COME BACK HOME MY LITTLE CHICKS." 2. MAGNETIC TEMPO WORDS. 3. TEACHER SELECTED TEMPO LISTENING MATERIAL WITH WORKSHEETS. 4. PENCILS.

PROCEDURE;
1. GREETING; sung as Hel-   child-   (class)   Hel-   teach-
                         lo   dren.   lo   er.

2. OPENING SONG; "In and Out." On this they will'
   a. Sing the words and clap the beat.
   b. Do some form of part work.

STATE OBJECTIVES;

3. NEW SONG; "Come Back Home My Little Chicks." On this they will;
   a. Learn the song by rote.
   b. Clap the beat while singing the words.
   c. Clap the way the words go.
   d. Use hands to show contour of the pitch.
   e. Use inner hearing to internalize the song.
   f. Teacher sings question. Class sings answer. Switch parts. Divide the class into question or answer. Switch parts.
(BEHAVIORAL OBJECTIVE 1)

4. PRESENT TEMPO; method of presentation;
   a. Define tempo.
   b. Teacher explains that there are words that tell when the music is fast or slow. Places the word tempo at the top of the magnetic board. Places the word fast on the left side of the magnetic board. Places the word slow on the right side of the board. Places and pronounces the tempo words that are in the fast family under the word fast. Places and pronounces the tempo words in the slow family under the word slow. Teacher pronounces the words again. This time the class repeats after the teacher. A discussion on rate of speed may be appropriate at this point.
(BEHAVIORAL OBJECTIVE 2)

5. LISTENING ACTIVITY; Teacher selects method of presentation.
(BEHAVIORAL OBJECTIVE 3)

6. CLOSURE; 1. Name the new song learned today. 2. Define tempo.

7. GOOD-BYE; sung as; Good-   child-   (class) Good-   teach-
                               bye   dren.   bye   er.

WRITE ON BOARD; 1. LEARN A NEW SONG. 2. LEARN ABOUT TEMPO.

COME BACK HOME MY LITTLE CHICKS

QUESTION

4	s	s	m	m	s	s	m
4	Come	back	home	my	lit-	tle	chicks?

s	m
Why	not?

s	m
Of	What?

s	s	m	m
Where's he	hid-	ing?	

s	s	m	m	s	m
What's	he	drying	his	face	on?

ANSWER

s	s	m
We	won't	come!

s	s	m
We're	a-	fraid!

s	s	m
Of	the	wolf.

s	s	m
In	the	woods.

(wait)

(SPOKEN) ON THE KITTY CAT TAIL!

LESSON 6 GRADE_____ TEACHER_____

LESSON 7
INSTRUCTIONAL OBJECTIVES;
1. PREPARE so la mi.
2. PRESENT the beat and its properties.
3. PRACTICE applying beat properties.

BEHAVIORAL OBJECTIVES; students will;
1. Learn a new song. (INSTRUCTIONAL OBJECTIVE 1)
2. Learn about time signature, measure, bar line, and double bar line. (INSTRUCTIONAL OBJECTIVE 2)
3. Apply those things learned about the beat. (INSTRUCTIONAL OBJECTIVE 3)

MATERIALS; 1. SONG; "LUCY LOCKETT." 2. TIME SIGNATURE, MEASURE, BAR LINE AND DOUBLE BAR LINE FLASH CARDS.

PROCEDURE;

lo
1. GREETING;(NEW) sung as; Hel-   to   (class echoes the same.)
                                                    you.

2. OPENING SONG; "Come Back Home My Little Chicks." On this they will;
   a. Sing the words and clap the beat.
   b. Do some form of part work.

STATE OBJECTIVES;

3. NEW SONG; "Lucy Lockett." On this they will;
   a. Learn the song by rote.
   b. Clap the beat while singing the words.
   c. Clap the way the words go.
   d. Use hands to show contour of pitch.
   e. Use inner hearing to internalize the song.
(BEHAVIORAL OBJECTIVE 1)

4. PRESENT THE BEAT AND ITS PROPERTIES; write the following on the board.
   a. A time signature tells how many beats are in a measure.
      (The heart is used to represent the word beat. Later the heart will be replaced with the beat note and the number representing the beat note.)

2 two	3 three	4 four
♥ beats in a measure	♥ beats in a measure	♥ beats in a measure

b. A measure is the space between two bar lines.

| measure | measure | measure |

c. a bar line separates the music into measures.

bar line   bar line   bar line

d. A double bar line is placed at the end of the music.

(ERASE BOARD)
(BEHAVIORAL OBJECTIVE 2)

5. APPLICATION; Teacher gives students an opportunity to identify each sign from flash cards. Assigns students to write a given sign on the chalkboard. Draws hearts and a time signature. Assigns a student to place bar lines.
(BEHAVIORAL OBJECTIVE 3)

6. CLOSURE; 1. Name the new song learned today. 2. Define; time signature, measure, bar line, and double bar line.

7. GOOD-BYE; sung as; Good-   bye   to   you.   (class echoes the same.)

WRITE ON BOARD; 1. LEARN A NEW SONG. 2. LEARN ABOUT THE BEAT AND ITS PROPERTIES.

LUCY LOCKETT

2	s	s	l	l	s	s	m	m	s	s	l	l	s	m
4	Lu-	cy	Lock-	et	lost	her	pock-	et	Kit-	ty	Fish-	er	found	it.

	s	s	l	l	s	s	m	m	s	s	l	l	s	m
	Not	a	pen-	ny	was	there	in	it	on-	ly	rib-	bon	round	it.

GAME;
1. Children are seated in a circle.
2. One child walks around inside the circle and carries the pocket while all sing.
3. The pocket is dropped in front of a child in the circle.
4. The child picks up the pocket and a chase ensues to get to the vacant place before being touched.
5. Whatever the outcome the game begins again.

LESSON 7 GRADE_____ TEACHER_____

TERMINAL 1 AFTER LESSON 7

BEHAVIORAL OBJECTIVES; students will complete a worksheet that will include the following.
1. Defining music terms.
2. Identifying rhythm signs.
3. Naming music symbols.

MATERIALS; 1. TERMINAL 1 WORKSHEETS AND PENCILS. 2. OVERHEAD AND TRANSPARENCY OF TERMINAL 1 WORKSHEET.

PROCEDURE;
1. GREETING; sung as; Hel-   lo   to   you.   (class echoes the same.)
                        s   1   s   m
                        ta   ta   ta   ta

2. OPENING SONG; "Lucy Lockett." On this they will;
   a. Sing the words and clap the beat.
   b. Do some form of part work.

SPONGE ACTIVITY;

STATE OBJECTIVES;

3. WORKSHEET ACTIVITY;
   a. Worksheets are distributed.
   b. Teacher uses overhead to review what is on the worksheets and how to fill in the spaces in front of the numbers with the matching letter.
   c. Pencils are passed out and students fill in worksheets independently.
(BEHAVIORAL OBJECTIVES 1, 2, AND 3)

4. PLAY PARTY; LUCY LOCKETT. (NEW)

5. GOOD-BYE; sung as; Good-   bye   to   you.   (class echoes the same.)
                      s   1   s   m
                      ta   ta   ta   ta

WRITE ON BOARD; 1. FILL IN A WORKSHEET

TERMINAL 1   GRADE_____ TEACHER_____

18

Match the words or signs with the letter that describes what it is.

_____ 1. Music

a. The space between two bar lines.

_____ 2. Beat

b. The loudness or softness of music.

_____ 3. Pitch

c. The repeated pulse of the music.

_____ 4. Dynamics

d. Divides the music into measures.

_____ 5. 2 3 4

e. The speed of the music.

_____ 6. Bar line

f. The art of sound in time.

_____ 7. Measure

g. The highness or lowness of a sound.

_____ 8. Double bar line

h. Time signatures.

_____ 9. Tempo

i. The longness or shortness of a sound.

_____ 10. Rhythm

j. Placed at the end of the music.

TERMINAL 1 WORKSHEET NO. ONE OF ONE.

LESSON 8

INSTRUCTIONAL OBJECTIVES;
1. PREPARE so la mi.
2. PRESENT ta, titi, quarter note, and two eighth notes.
3. PRESENT singing rhythm syllables.

BEHAVIORAL OBJECTIVES; students will;
1. Learn a new song. (INSTRUCTIONAL OBJECTIVE 1)
2. Learn two rhythm signs and their syllables. (INSTRUCTIONAL OBJECTIVE 2)
3. Learn to sing the rhythm syllables of a song. (INSTRUCTIONAL OBJECTIVE 3)

MATERIALS; 1. SONG; "BOUNCE HIGH." 2. MAGNETIC BOARD. 3. MAGNETIC TA AND TITI SIGNS. 4. MAGNETIC WORDS FOR "BEE, BEE." 5. MAGNETIC HEARTS.

PROCEDURE;

1. GREETING; sung as;   Hel-   lo   to   you.   (class echoes the same.)

2. OPENING SONG; "Lucy Lockett." On this they will;
   a. Sing the words and clap the beat.
   b. Do some form of part work.

STATE OBJECTIVES;

3. NEW SONG; "Bounce High, Bounce Low." On this they will;
   a. Learn the song by rote.
   b. Clap the beat while singing the words.
   c. Clap the way the words go.
   d. Use hands to show contour of pitch.
   e. Use inner hearing to internalize the song.
   (BEHAVIORAL OBJECTIVE 1)

4. PRESENT THE QUARTER NOTE AND TWO EIGHT NOTES;
   Presentation rhyme "Bee, Bee."
   a. Class claps the beat and says the rhyme.
   b. Teacher places words on the magnetic board.
   c. Class helps teacher place hearts under words that come with a beat.
      DEFINE NOTE IN RELATIONSHIP TO RHYTHM
   d. Teacher explains that each heart that has one sound will be replaced with a note stem. The stem stands for a quarter note. (Note is drawn on board.) The spoken rhythm syllable is ta. (Teacher replaces hearts that have one sound with ta signs.)
   e. When there are two sounds for one beat, two stems connected with a beam is used. These stems stand for two eighth notes. (Notes are drawn on board.) The spoken rhythm syllable is titi. (Teacher replaces hearts that have two sounds with titi signs.)

    f. Teacher demonstrates how to clap and speak the rhythm. Then demonstrates how to clap the beat and speak the rhythm. Students are given an opportunity to do the same.
(BEHAVIORAL OBJECTIVE 2)

5. RHYTHM OF A SONG; Presentation song "Rain, Rain."
    a. Class sings song.
    b. Teacher helps class derive the rhythm.
    c. Teacher writes rhythm on the board.
    d. Class sings rhythm syllables again.
    e. Teacher helps class derive and write rhythm of other familiar songs.
(BEHAVIORAL OBJECTIVE 3)

6. CLOSURE; 1. Name the new song learned today. 2. Name the two rhythm signs learned today and tell something about them.

                        bye
2. GOOD-BYE; sung as; Good-   to   (class echoes the same.)
                                you.

WRITE ON BOARD; 1. LEARN A NEW SONG. 2. LEARN TWO RHYTHM SIGNS. 3. LEARN TO SING THE RHYTHM SYLLABLES OF A SONG.

BOUNCE HIGH, BOUNCE LOW

2	s	1	s	m	s	s	1	1	s	m
4	Bounce	high,	bounce	low,	bounce	the	ball	to	shi-	loh.

BOUNCE BALL AS; 1. Bounce catch, bounce catch one child at a time.
                    2. Two children face each other with enough space between them to bounce the ball on the floor to the child across from them.

LESSON 8 GRADE_____ TEACHER_____

LESSON 9
INSTRUCTIONAL OBJECTIVES;
1. PREPARE do.
2. PRESENT the quarter rest.
3. PRACTICE ta and titi.

BEHAVIORAL OBJECTIVES; students will;
1. Learn two new songs. (INSTRUCTIONAL OBJECTIVE 1)
2. Learn a new rhythm sign. (INSTRUCTIONAL OBJECTIVE 2)
3. Write the rhythm for several rhymes. (INSTRUCTIONAL OBJECTIVE 3)

MATERIALS; 1. SONGS; "PEAS PORRIDGE," AND "RING AROUND THE ROSIE."
2. WORKSHEET WITH SEVERAL FAMILIAR RHYMES. 3. OVERHEAD PROJECTOR AND
WORKSHEET TRANSPARENCY.

PROCEDURE;
                             lo
1. GREETING; sung as; Hel-   to   (class echoes the same.)
                                       you.

2. OPENING SONG; "Bounce High, Bounce Low." On this they will;
   a. Sing the words and clap the beat.
   b. Do some form of part work.

STATE OBJECTIVES;

3. NEW SONGS; "Peas Porridge," and "Ring Around The Rosie." On these they will;
   a. Learn the songs by rote.
   b. Clap the beat and sing the words.
   c. Clap the way the words go.
   d. Use inner hearing to internalize the song.
(BEHAVIORAL OBJECTIVE 1.)

4. PRESENT THE QUARTER REST; Presentation song "In And Out."
   a. Class sings song.
   b. Derives the rhythm.
   c. Teacher writes the following on the board:
      i. The time signature is written as a four with a heart under it.
      ii. The rhythm is written in stem notation of four lines. First, second and fourth
         lines as ta, ta, ta.
         The third line is written ta, ta, ta, ta.
   d. Assign a student to place the hearts under the rhythm and tell why it is placed
      there. (example; one sound for one beat.)

PAGE 2 LESSON 9

    e. Class claps the beat and sings the song. They discover there is a beat at the end of the lines 1, 2 and 4 but no sound. The teacher places a beat at the end of these lines and explains that sometimes there is a beat, but no sound. When this happens, a rest appears in the music. (Teacher writes a quarter rest over the beats at the end of the lines 1, 2, and 4.) The name quarter rest is given and the open hand is shown. This means no sound for one beat.

    f. Teacher claps the beat and sings the rhythm syllables. Class does the same.
(BEHAVIORAL OBJECTIVE 2)

5. TRANSITION-STUDENT PERFORMANCE;
    a. Students clap the beat and say the words for "Queen, Queen" and "Engine, Engine."
    b. Students will clap the way the words go then clap and recite the rhythm syllables.

6. WRITING ACTIVITY; Worksheets and pencils are distributed. Teacher places a transparency worksheet on the overhead and helps students write the rhythm over the words.
(BEHAVIORAL OBJECTIVE 3)

7. CLOSURE; 1. Name the new song learned today. 2. Name the new rhythm sign learned today. 3. What is ta? 4. What is titi?

8. GOOD-BYE; sung as; Good- bye to you. (class echoes the same.)

WRITE ON BOARD; 1. LEARN TWO NEW SONGS. 2. LEARN A NEW RHYTHM SIGN.
3. REVIEW TA AND TITI.

PEAS PORRIDGE HOT

2. Some like it hot, some like it cold.
    Some like it in a pot nine days old.

RING AROUND THE ROSIE

```
2   s      s      m      l        s       m        s      s      m      l
4  Ring    a-   round   the      ro-     sy       pock-  et    full    of


    s             m                s               m        s                m
    po-          sy               Ash-            es,      ash-             es


    s             s                d
    all          fall            down.
```

NAME _____ CLASS _____ DATE _____

WRITE THE RHYTHM OVER THE WORDS AS TA ⌐, OR TITI ⊓

QUEEN QUEEN

Queen,	Queen	Ca- ro-	line.
Washed her	hair in	tur- pen-	tine.
Tur- pen-	tine	made it	shine.
Queen,	Queen	Ca- ro-	line.

ENGINE, ENGINE

En- gine,	en- gine	num- ber	nine.
Go- ing	down Chi-	ca- go	line.
If that	train should	jump the	track.
Do you	want your	mon- ey	back?

PAGE 1 LESSON 9 WORKSHEET

TWO, FOUR, SIX, EIGHT

TWO,	FOUR,	SIX,	EIGHT.
Meet me	at the	gar- den	gate.
If I'm	late	don't	wait.
TWO,	FOUR,	SIX,	EIGHT.

BEE, BEE BUMBLE BEE

Bee,	bee,	bum- ble	bee.
Stung a	man up-	on his	knee.
Stung a	pig up-	on his	snout.
I de-	clare that	you are	out.

TERMINAL 2 AFTER LESSON 9

INSTRUCTION OBJECTIVES;
1. PREPARE the skill of taking dictation.
2. PRESENT the method of taking dictation.
3. PRACTICE taking dictation.
4. Fill in a worksheet.

BEHAVIORAL OBJECTIVES; students will;
1. Use rhythm manipulatives to create rhythm patterns.
   (INSTRUCTIONAL OBJECTIVE 1)
2. Learn to take rhythm dictation. (INSTRUCTIONAL OBJECTIVE 2)
3. Take rhythm dictation. (INSTRUCTIONAL OBJECTIVE 3)
4. Identify music terms, signs, and symbols. (INSTRUCTIONAL OBJECTIVE 4)

MATERIALS; 1. RHYTHM MANIPULATIVES. 2. PENCILS AND TERMINAL 2 WORKSHEETS.
3. FLASH CARDS.

PROCEDURE;

1. GREETING; sung as; Hel-   lo   to   you.   (class echoes the same.)

2. OPENING SONGS; "Peas Porridge Hot," and "Ring Around the Rosie."
   On these they will;
   a. Sing the words and clap the beat.
   b. Sing and clap the rhythm.
   c. Sing the rhythm and clap the beat.

SPONGE ACTIVITY;

STATE OBJECTIVES;

3. Students will use ta, titi, and quarter rest rhythm manipulatives to create rhythm
   patterns.
(BEHAVIORAL OBJECTIVE 1)

4. Teacher will model how to take dictation.
(BEHAVIORAL OBJECTIVE 2)

5. Pencils and paper will be passed out and students will take dictation.
(BEHAVIORAL OBJECTIVE 3)

6. WORKSHEET ACTIVITY; Distribute Terminal 2 worksheets. Teacher uses over head
   to explain how to fill in the answers. Students are given an opportunity to individually
   fill in the worksheet
(BEHAVIORAL OBJECTIVE 4)

27

7. CLOSURE; Students will clap rhythm from flash cards. (NEW)

8. GOOD-BYE; sung as; Good-   bye   to   you.   (class echoes the same.)
                                     s   1   s   m
                                  ta   ta   ta   ta

WRITE ON BOARD; 1. LEARN TO CREATE RHYTHM PATTERNS. 2. LEARN ABOUT TAKING DICTATION. 3. TAKE DICTATION.

NAME _____ CLASS _____ DATE_____

1. _____

2. _____

3. _____

4. _____

5. _____

6. _____

7. _____

8 _____

9. _____

10._____

TERMINAL 2 WORKSHEET NO. ONE OF TWO.

NAME _____ CLASS _____ DATE _____

Match the words or signs with the letter that describes them.

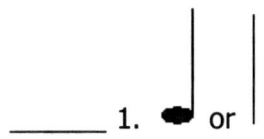

_____ 1. ♩ or | A. The tune of a song.

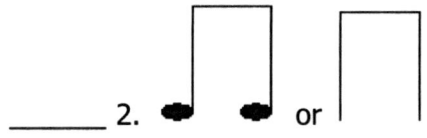

_____ 2. ♫ or ⊓   B. Signs for musical silence.

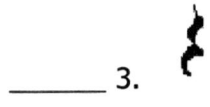

_____ 3. 𝄽   C. The shape of the melody.

_____ 4. Rests   D. Quarter rest. No sound for one beat.

_____ 5. Notes   E. Two eighth notes or titi. Two sounds for one beat.

_____ 6. Contour   F. Quarter note or ta. One sound for the beat.

_____ 7. Melody   G. Signs for musical sound.

TERMINAL 2 WORKSHEET NO. TWO OF TWO.

LESSON 10

INSTRUCTIONAL OBJECTIVES;
1. PREPARE re.
2. PRESENT so mi on the tone ladder.
3. PRACTICE ta, titi, and the quarter rest.

BEHAVIORAL OBJECTIVES;
1. Learn a new song. (INSTRUCTIONAL OBJECTIVE 1)
2. Learn two pitch syllables and their hand signs. (INSTRUCTIONAL OBJECTIVE 2)
3. Aurally identify ta, titi, and quarter rest in familiar songs.
   (INSTRUCTIONAL OBJECTIVE 3)

MATERIALS; 1. SONG; "HOT CROSS BUNS." 2. MAGNETIC SO AND MI FOR TONE
LADDER. TA, TITI, AND QUARTER REST FLASH CARDS.

PROCEDURE;

1. GREETING; sung as; Hel- lo to you. (class echoes the same.)

2. OPENING SONGS; "Peas Porridge Hot," and "Ring Around The Rosie."
   On these they will;
   a. Sing the words and clap the beat.
   b. Do some form of part work.

3. FLASH CARD ACTIVITY;
   Known rhythm signs.

STATE OBJECTIVES;

4. NEW SONG; "Hot Cross Buns." On this they will;
   a. Learn the song by rote.
   b. Clap the beat and sing the words.
   c. Clap the way the words go.
   d. Use inner hearing to internalize the song.
(BEHAVIORAL OBJECTIVE 1)

5. PRESENT SO AND MI ON THE TONE LADDER.
   Presentation song "Rain, Rain."
   a. Class sings song.
   b. Teacher writes the melodic contour on the board using high and low dashes.
      (review definition of contour.)
   c. Teacher: "We can sing the melodic contour of a song with pitch syllables. The
      syllable for the high sound is so. The syllable for the low sound is mi. I will sing
      the song using syllables." (Teacher sings and writes the syllable letters on the
      dashes.)

    d. Class sings syllables the same as the teacher did.

    e. Teacher: "There is a hand sign for each of these syllables. The hand sign for so is"... (teacher gives sign.) "The hand sign for mi is"... (teacher gives sign.)

    f. Teacher sings the syllables and makes the hand signs. Class does the same.

    g. Attention is called to the tone ladder and the hand sign chart. So and mi on the hand sign chart and the so and mi hand signs are turned over on the hand sign ladder.

(BEHAVIORAL OBJECTIVE 2)

6. RHYTHM STUDY; (Review the definition of rhythm.)
    Presentation songs; "Pease Porridge Hot", and "Lucy Lockett."

    a. Class sings songs.

    b. Derives the rhythm by clapping and singing the rhythm syllables.

    c. Teacher or student writes the rhythm on the board.

    d. Student is assigned to place heart beats and tell why they are placed with that rhythm sign. (i.e. one sound for one beat etc.)

BEHAVIORAL OBJECTIVE 3)

7. CLOSURE; 1. Name the new song learned today. 2. Name the pitch syllables learned today and make the hand sign for each one.

                      bye

8. GOOD-BYE; sung as; Good-   to   (class echoes the same.)

                                       you.

WRITE ON BOARD; 1. LEARN A NEW SONG. 2. LEARN TWO PITCH SYLLABLES. 3. REVIEW TA, TITI, AND THE QUARTER REST.

HOT CROSS BUNS

m	r	d	𝄽
Hot	cross	buns.	

m	r	d	𝄽
Hot	cross	buns.	

d d	d d	r r	r r
One a	pen- ny	two a	pen- ny

m	r	d	𝄽
Hot	cross	buns.	

LESSON 11
INSTRUCTIONAL OBJECTIVES;
1. PREPARE (a) la. (b) re (c) accent.
2. PRESENT (a) The staff. (b) repeat sign.
3. PRACTICE deriving rhythm.

BEHAVIORAL OBJECTIVES; students will;
1. Learn two new songs. (INSTRUCTIONAL OBJECTIVE 1)
2. Learn two music symbols. (INSTRUCTIONAL OBJECTIVE 2)
3. Derive the rhythm of a familiar song. (INSTRUCTIONAL OBJECTIVE 3)

MATERIALS; 1. SONGS; "SNAIL, SNAIL", AND "BOW, WOW, WOW". 2. STUDENT STAFF
CHALK BOARDS, CHALK AND ERASERS. 3. A BALL. 4. STAFF LINER.

PROCEDURE;
1. GREETING; sung as;   Hel-   to   (class echoes the same.)
                      s   lo   s   you.   (class echoes with hand
                            m   m   signs and pitch names.)

2. OPENING SONG; "Hot Cross Buns." On this they will;
    a. Sing the words and clap the beat.
    b. Do some form of part work.

3. FLASH CARD ACTIVITY; Select one or both.
___ a. Known rhythm signs.

___ b. Known solfege/ rhythm cards.

STATE OBJECTIVES;

4. NEW SONGS; "Snail, Snail", and "Bow, Wow, Wow". On these they will;
    a. Learn the songs by rote.
    b. Clap the beat while singing the words.
    c. Clap the way the words go.
    d. Use inner hearing to internalize the song.
(BEHAVIORAL OBJECTIVE 1)

5. PRESENT THE STAFF; method of presentation board illustration.
    a. Teacher uses the staff liner to draw a staff.
    b. Teacher tells students;
        i.   This is a staff.
        ii. A staff is what music is written on.
        iii. A staff has five lines and four spaces.
        iv. The lines and spaces are counted from the bottom to the top.
    c. Teacher models how to count lines and then how to count spaces.

  d. Chalk, staff chalk boards, and erasers are distributed. Rules are given for using these materials. Students are given an exercise on numbering the lines and spaces. Emphasize; ON THE LINE and IN THE SPACE. Materials are taken up.
(BEHAVIORAL OBJECTIVE 2 INCOMPLETE)

6. RHYTHM STUDY; Presentation song "Bounce High, Bounce Low."
  a. Class sings song.
  b. Derives rhythm by singing the rhythm syllables.
  c. Rhythm is written on the board.
  d. Teacher writes the time signature.
  e. One student is assigned to write the beats. Another is assigned to draw in the bar lines, and the double bar line.
(BEHAVIORAL OBJECTIVE 3)

7. PRESENT REPEAT SIGN;
  a. Teacher: "Suppose we want to sing this song twice but no one says sing again. What can we do?"
  b. Class is given time to give answer.
  c. Teacher: "There is a music sign that tells us to sing or play the music again. Look on the Universal music board and see if you can find a sign that tells us to do it again."
  d. After the sign is found, the teacher writes it at the end of the rhythm that is on the board.
  e. Class claps the beat and sings the rhythm syllables, this time observing the repeat sign.
(BEHAVIORAL OBJECTIVE 2 COMPLETE)

8. CHANGE OF PACE; BOUNCE HIGH BOUNCE LOW PLAY PARTY. (NEW)

9. CLOSURE; 1. Name the new songs learned today. 2. Review the purpose of a staff and a repeat sign.

10. GOOD-BYE; sung as; Good-   to   (class echoes the same.)
            bye   you.   (use hand signs and pitch names.)

PAGE 3 LESSON 11

WRITE ON BOARD; 1. LEARN A NEW SONG. 2. LEARN TWO MUSIC SIGNS. 3. DERIVE THE RHYTHM OF A FAMILIAR SONG.

SNAIL, SNAIL

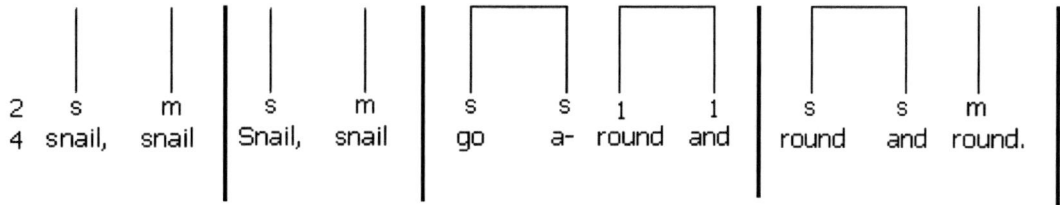

GAME; Line formation.
1. Designate beginning and end person.
2. The beginning person stands still while all follow the end person in a wide circle.
3. At some point the end person goes in the opposite direction. All follow and possibly unwind.

BOW, WOW, WOW

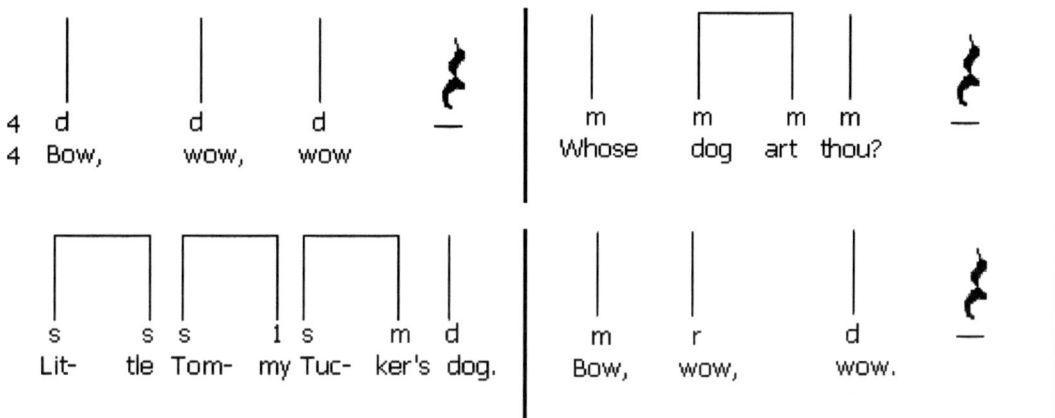

GAME; Formation; circle and face partner.
1. On "Bow, wow, wow," stamp feet three times.
2. On "Whose dog art thou?" shake finger at partner.
3. On "Little Tommy Tucker's dog," change place with partner. After change still face partner.
4. On last "Bow, wow, wow," stamp feet three times.
5. Turn quickly to a new partner. Game begins again.

LESSON 11 GRADE_____ TEACHER_____

36

LESSON 12
INSTRUCTIONAL OBJECTIVES;
1. PREPARE the half note.
2. PRESENT (a) La on the tone ladder. (b) Accent as a music sign.

BEHAVIORAL OBJECTIVES; students will;
1. Learn a new song. (INSTRUCTIONAL OBJECTIVE 1)
2. Learn a new pitch syllable and its hand sign. (INSTRUCTIONAL OBJECTIVE 2)
3. Learn a new music sign. (INSTRUCTIONAL OBJECTIVE 3)

MATERIALS; 1. SONG; "WHO'S THAT?" 2. MAGNETIC LA FOR THE TONE LADDER. 3. A BALL. 4. ACCENT SIGN ON UNIVERSAL LANGUAGE BOARD.

PROCEDURE;
1. GREETING; sung as;   Hel-   lo   to   you.   (class echoes the same.)

2. OPENING SONGS; "Snail, Snail", and "Bow, Wow, Wow". On these they will;
    a. Sing the words and clap the beat.
    b. Do some form of part work.

3. FLASH CARD ACTIVITY; Select one or both.
    ___ a. Known rhythm signs.

    ___ b. Known solfege / rhythm cards.

STATE OBJECTIVES;

4. NEW SONG; "Who's that?" On this they will;
    a. Learn the song by rote.
    b. Clap the beat while singing the words.
    c. Clap the way the words go.
    d. Use inner hearing to internalize the song.
(BEHAVIORAL OBJECTIVE 1)

5. PRESENT LA ON THE TONE LADDER; Presentation song, "Lucy Lockett".
    a. Class sings song.
    b. Derives rhythm by singing and clapping the rhythm syllables. Teacher writes the rhythm on the board.
    c. Follow direction for DERIVING MELODY OF A SONG WITH ONE UNKNOWN TONE. After the unknown tone is identified the name is given as la and the hand sign is shown.
    d. Class sings "Lucy Lockett" using hand signs and then on the tone ladder.
    e. Same procedure may be followed using "Snail, Snail."
(BEHAVIORAL OBJECTIVE 2)

6. PRESENT THE ACCENT; Presentation song "Bounce High."
    a. Class signs song with words and then with rhythm syllables.
    b. Rhythm is written on the board with bar lines.
    c. Class sings rhythm again while the teacher bounces a ball on the first beat of each measure.
    d. Teacher: "Class we can write the sound of the ball under the rhythm sign that it comes with. There is a sign that tells us to sing the word louder than the others."
    e. Class is given time to find the sign on the Universal Language board.
    f. After the sign is found, the name is given as accent. Accent is defined.
    g. Teacher places an accent under rhythm signs that come with the bounce of the ball.
    h. Class sings song. A student bounces the ball. A student points to the accents.
(BEHAVIORAL OBJECTIVE 3)

7. CHANGE OF PACE; BOW, WOW, WOW PLAY PARTY. (NEW)

8. CLOSURE; 1. Name the new song learned today. 2. Tell something about the new pitch syllable learned today. 3. Name the new music sign learned today.

9. GOOD-BYE; this time sing the words, pitch syllables and syllables and hand signs.

              bye
1. Good-   to   (class echoes)
                        you.

              1
2.   s   s   (class echoes)
                      m

3. Teacher sings number #2 again with hand signs. Class does the same.

PAGE 3 LESSON 12

WRITE ON BOARD; 1. LEARN A NEW SONG. 2. LEARN A NEW PITCH SYLLABLE 3. LEARN A NEW MUSIC SIGN.

WHO'S THAT

| 2 | d | s | r r m m | r d |
| 4 | Who's | that | tap- ping at the | win- dow? |

| | d | s | r r m m | d |
| | Who's | that | knock- ing at the | door? |

| | d | s | r r m m | r d |
| | Mom- | my's | tap- ping at the | win- dow? |

| | d | s | r r m m | d |
| | Dad- | dy's | knock- ing at the | door? |

NAME PLAY; Substitute children's names for mommy and daddy.

LESSON 13
INSTRUCTIONAL OBJECTIVES
1. PREPARE (a) re. (b) The half note.
2. PRESENT so and mi on the staff.
3. PRACTICE writing so and mi on the staff.

BEHAVIORAL OBJECTIVES; students will;
1. Learn a new song. (INSTRUCTIONAL OBJECTIVE 1)
2. Derive a generalization statement for so and mi. (INSTRUCTIONAL OBJECTIVE 2)
3. Write so and mi on the staff. (INSTRUCTIONAL OBJECTIVE 3)

MATERIALS; 1. SONG; "HERE COMES A BLUE BIRD". 2. BIG CHART WITH SO MI ON THE STAFF. 3. FLANNEL BOARDS PELON STAFFS AND FELT CIRCLES. 4. MAGNETIC BOARD AND MAGNETIC DISCS.

PROCEDURE;

1. GREETING; sung as; Hel-   lo   to   you.   (use syllables and hand signs.)

2. OPENING SONG; "Who's That?" On this they will;
   a. Sing the words and clap the beat.
   b. Do some form of part work.

3. FLASH CARD ACTIVITY; Select one or both.

___ a. Known rhythm signs.

___ b. Known solfege / rhythm cards.

STATE OBJECTIVES;

4. NEW SONG; "Here Comes a Blue Bird." On this they will;
   a. Learn the song by rote.
   b. Clap the beat while singing the words.
   c. Clap the way the words go.
   d. Use inner hearing to internalize the song.
(BEHAVIORAL OBJECTIVE 1)

   TRANSITION; Class will sing all songs learned to prepare so mi. On these they will;
   e. Clap the beat while singing the words.
   f. Sing the pitch syllables and make the hand signs.

5. PRESENT SO AND MI ON THE STAFF; method of presentation;
   a. Teacher sings a line-line so mi exercise from the big chart and points to each note. Then teacher sings a space-space so mi exercise from the big chart and points to each note.
   b. Teacher leads the class into a discussion resulting in the discovery that when so is on a line, mi is on the line below it. When so is in a space, mi is in the space below it.
   c. Class sings the exercises using pitch syllables and then pitch syllables with hand signs.

(BEHAVIORAL OBJECTIVE 2)

6. WRITING ACTIVITY; method of procedure;
   a. Teacher distributes flannel boards, pelon staffs, and four felt circles. Rules are given for using these materials.
   b. Students are told to lay the staff on the flannel board.
   c. Class states so mi rule. Teacher tells students what line or space to place so on. Then tells them what line or space to place so on and they are to place mi on the correct line or space under it. Teacher places the correct placement on the magnetic board so class can check answers. Materials are taken up.

(BEHAVIORAL OBJECTIVE 3)

7. CHANGE OF PACE; BOW, WOW, WOW PLAY PARTY.

8. CLOSURE; 1. Name the new song learned today. 2. State the generalization statement for so and mi.

9. GOOD-BYE; sung as; Good- bye to you. (syllables and hand signs also)

41

PAGE 3 LESSON 13

WRITE ON BOARD; 1. LEARN A NEW SONG. 2. PLACE SO AND MI ON THE STAFF.

HERE COMES A BLUEBIRD

2 s	s	1	s	m	s	s	1	s	m
4 Here	comes	a	blue-	bird	in	through	my	win-	dow.

m	r	r	r	r	d	m	d
Hey.	dee-	dle	dum	a	day,	day,	day.

s	s	s	1	s	m	s	s	1	s	m
Take	a	lit-	tle	part-	ner	hop	in	the	gar-	den.

m	r	r	r	r	d	m	d
Hey.	dee-	dle	dum	a	day,	day,	day.

GAME; Formation; Children stand in a circle facing partners with hands joined to form a window.
1. One child is the bluebird.
2. All sing as the blue bird weaves in and out of the windows.
3. On "Take a little partner," all swing partners. The bluebird takes someone's partner.
4. The child left without a partner becomes the new bluebird and the game begins again.

LESSON 13 GRADE_____ TEACHER_____

TERMINAL 3 AFTER LESSON 13

BEHAVIORAL OBJECTIVES; students will;
1. Write six so mi patterns on the staff.
2. Write a familiar so mi song on the staff.
3. Write an original eight measure composition.

MATERIALS; 1. TERMINAL 3 WORKSHEETS AND PENCILS. 2. OVERHEAD AND
TRANSPARENCIES FOR TERMINAL 3 WORKSHEETS. 3. FLASH CARDS.

PROCEDURES;
1. GREETING; sung as; Hel-   lo   to   you.   (class echoes the same.)
                         s   1   s   m
                         ta   ta   ta   ta

2. OPENING SONGS; "Here comes a Blue Bird." On this they will;
    a. Sing the words and clap the beat.
    b. Do some form of part work.

SPONGE ACTIVITY;

STATE OBJECTIVES;

3. WRITING ACTIVITY 1; Method of procedure;
    a. Distribute six so mi worksheets.
    b. Teacher uses overhead and discusses heading and how to fill out the worksheets.
        Transparency is removed.
    c. Pencils are distributed and students fill out worksheets independently.
(BEHAVIORAL OBJECTIVE 1).

4. WRITING ACTIVITY 2; Same method of procedure as 1 except distribute familiar song
    worksheets.
(BEHAVIORAL OBJECTIVE 2)

5. WRITING ACTIVITY 3; Same method of procedure as 1 and 2 except distribute
    original composition worksheets.
(BEHAVIORAL OBJECTIVE 3)

6. CLOSURE; flash cards.

7. PLAY PARTIES; familiar ones.

8. GOOD-BYE; sung as; Good-   bye   to   you.   (class echoes the same.)
                              s   1   s   m
                              ta   ta   ta   ta

WRITE ON BOARD; 1. WRITE SIX SO MI PATTERNS ON THE STAFF. 2. WRITE A FAMILIAR SO MI SONG ON THE STAFF. 3. WRITE AN ORIGINAL EIGHT MEASURE COMPOSITION.

SIX SO MI PATTERNS ON THE STAFF

1.

s   m

2.

s s   m

3.

m m   s

4.

s   s   m   m

5.

s   m   m

6.

m   s   s

TERMINAL 3 WORKSHEET NO. ONE OF THREE.

NAME _____ CLASS _____ DATE _____

"RAIN, RAIN" ON THE STAFF.

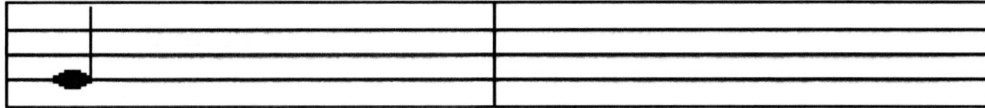

s   m   s   s   m

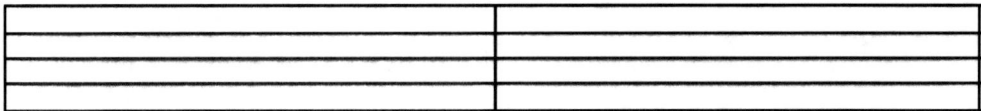

s   s   m   m   s   s   m

Match the name with the symbol.

___ 1.

a. Accent.

___ 2. <

b. Repeat.

___ 3. ‖:   :‖

c. Staff.

TERMINAL 3 WORKSHEET NO. TWO OF THREE.

WRITE AN ORIGINAL COMPOSITION;
1. Circle the top number of the time signature.
2. Write a letter under the staff for each note. Use a dash for the rest.
3. Write in the heart beats. Check time signature for number of beats in each measure

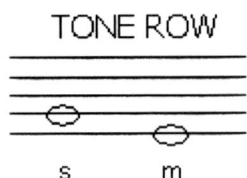

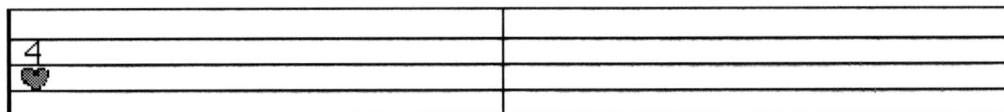

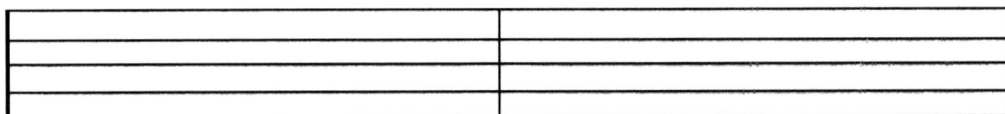

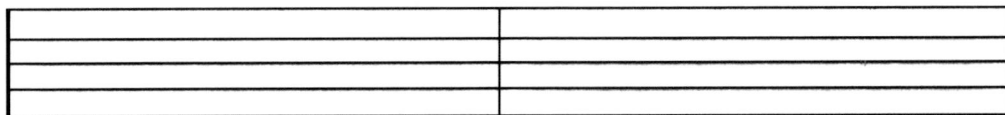

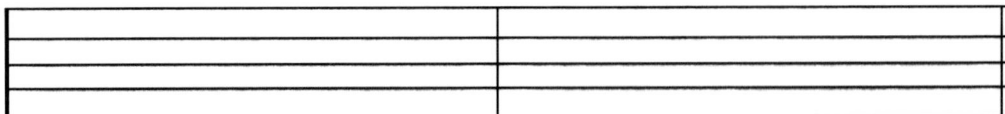

TONE ROW

s   m

RHYTHM SIGNS

TERMINAL 3 WORKSHEET NO. THREE OF THREE.

LESSON 14

INSTRUCTIONAL OBJECTIVES;
1. PREPARE do.
2. PRESENT the tie.
3. PRACTICE reading so and mi on the staff.

BEHAVIORAL OBJECTIVES; students will;
1. Learn a new song. (INSTRUCTIONAL OBJECTIVE 1)
2. Learn a new music sign. (INSTRUCTIONAL OBJECTIVE 2)
3. Review reading so and mi on the staff. (INSTRUCTIONAL OBJECTIVE 3)

MATERIALS; 1. SONG; "FUZZY WUZZY." 2. BIG CHART. 3. AN EXAMPLE OF THE TIE ON THE UNIVERSAL LANGUAGE BOARD. 4. FLASH CARDS.

PROCEDURE;
1. GREETING; sung as; Hel-   lo   to   you.   (Syllables and hand signs also.)
                      s   1   s   m

2. OPENING SONG; "Here Comes A Bluebird." On this they will;
   a. Sing the words and clap the beat.
   b. Do some form of part work.

3. FLASH CARD ACTIVITY; select one or both.
___ a. Known rhythm cards.

___ b. Known solfege / rhythm cards.

STATE OBJECTIVES;

4. NEW SONG; "Fuzzy Wuzzy." On this they will;
   a. Learn the song by rote.
   b. Clap the beat while singing the words.
   c. Clap and sing the rhythm syllables.
   d. Use inner hearing to internalize the song.
(BEHAVIORAL OBJECTIVE 1)

5. PRESENT THE TIE; presentation song "Who's That?"
   a. Class sings song.
   b. Teacher writes "who's" on the board. Sings the word and gives two beats. (question) How many sounds (words) did you hear? (ans.) One. (question) How many beats did you hear? (ans.) Two. Teacher places one heart under the word and the other heart aligned to the right of the first.
   c. Teacher: "We have learned that a beat has sound or no sound."
   d. (Pointing to the first beat) Does this beat have a sound? (ans.) Yes. (Pointing to the second beat) Does this beat have a sound? (answers will vary. Some will say no.)
   e. Place a rest over the second beat and sing the word again.

PAGE 2 LESSON 14

f. Lead the class to discover that the sound of "who's" lasts through the second beat.

g. Erase the rest and place a ta over the second beat. (question) How can we make these two ta's belong to "who's"? (answers will vary).

h. There is a music sign that connects one sound to two or more beats. (Students are given a chance to find this sign on the Universal Language board.)

i. When the sign is found, the teacher draws a curve line connecting the two tas. The name tie is given and the definition as; a curved line connecting two notes on the same pitch for two or more beats. The tie makes the sound longer. From "Who's That?" teacher writes "who's." From "Here Comes A Bluebird," "hey" and "day". Each word is to be written with two tas and a tie. Spoken as ta ah. Clapped as clap-slide.

(BEHAVIORAL OBJECTIVE 2)

6. READING ACTIVITY; Review the generalization statement for so and mi. Class reads several so mi exercises from the big chart.
(BEHAVIORAL OBJECTIVE 3)

7. CHANGE OF PACE; HERE COME A BLUEBIRD PLAY PARTY. (NEW)

8. CLOSURE; 1. Name the new song learned today. 2. Name the new music sign learned today. 3. State the so mi rule.

9. GOOD-BYE; sung as; Good- bye   to   you.   (syllables and hand signs also.)
                                 s   1   s   m

WRITE ON BOARD; 1. LEARN A NEW SONG. 2. LEARN A NEW MUSIC SIGN. 3. REVIEW READING SO MI ON THE STAFF.

FUZZY WUZZY

LESSON 15
INSTRUCTIONAL OBJECTIVES;
1. PREPARE the slur.
2. PRESENT the half note and the half rest.
3. PRACTICE writing so and mi on the staff.

BEHAVIORAL OBJECTIVES; students will;
1. Learn a new song. (INSTRUCTIONAL OBJECTIVE 1)
2. Learn two new rhythm signs. (INSTRUCTIONAL OBJECTIVE 2)
3. Write so mi patterns on the staff. (INSTRUCTIONAL OBJECTIVE 3)

MATERIALS; 1. SONG; "TEDDY BEAR." 2. HALF NOTE AND HALF REST ON THE RHYTHM
SIGN DISPLAY AREA. 3. FLASH CARDS. 4. STAFF LINER.

PROCEDURE;
1. GREETING; sung as; Hel- lo   to   you.   (class echoes the same.)
                         s   l   s   m
2. OPENING SONG; "Fuzzy Wuzzy." On this they will;
   a. Sing the words and clap the beat.
   b. Do some form of part work.

3. FLASH CARD ACTIVITY; select one or both.
___ a. Known rhythm cards.

___ b. Known solfege / rhythm cards.

STATE OBJECTIVES;

4. NEW SONG; "Teddy Bear." On this they will;
   a. Learn the song by rote.
   b. Clap the beat while singing the words.
   c. Clap the way the words go.
   d. Use inner hearing to internalize the song.
(BEHAVIORAL OBJECTIVE 1)

5. PRESENT THE HALF NOTE. Presentation song "Who's That?"
   a. Class sings song.
   b. Derives rhythm by singing the rhythm syllables. Rhythm is written on the board using the tie for long sounds.
   c. Teacher tells class that "who's" and "that" are long sounds. The tie makes them long. However, there is a shorter way to write one sound for two beats. Students are given time to find the sign on the rhythm display area. After the sign has been found, the tied notes are erased and replaced with a half note. The note name is given as half note. The hand clap is shown as clap-slide. The rhythm syllable is spoken as too-oo.

50

    d. Class sings and claps the rhythm syllables.

    e. Teacher erases the rhythm one or two signs at a time as the class sings the rhythm over and over until all the signs are erased. A student is then assigned to write the rhythm back on the board.

    f. THE HALF REST may be presented as a teacher made short rhythm exercise. The hand sign is given. The rhythm syllable is rest, rest. The definition is no sound for two beats.

(BEHAVIORAL OBJECTIVE 2)

6. WRITING ACTIVITY; Students will be given instructions on writing so mi patterns.

    a. Teacher tells students where to place so. (line or space)

    b. Give instruction about the stem on the correct side of the note head.

    c. Give instruction on writing the titi with note heads. Especially if the pattern has a so mi titi.

    d. Students will be given an opportunity to go to the board, draw a staff with the staff liner, and write a given so mi pattern.

(BEHAVIORAL OBJECTIVE 3)

7. CHANGE OF PACE; "BOW, WOW, WOW," AND "HERE COMES A BLUEBIRD" PLAY PARTIES.

8. CLOSURE; 1. Name the new song learned today. 2. Name the new rhythm signs learned today. 3. State the so mi rule.

9. GOOD-BYE; sung as; Good- bye   to   you.   (class echoes the same.)
                       s   1   s   m

WRITE ON BOARD; 1. LEARN A NEW SONG. 2. LEARN TWO NEW RHYTHM SIGNS.
3. WRITE SO MI PATTERNS ON THE STAFF.

TEDDY BEAR

TERMINAL 4 AFTER LESSON 15

BEHAVIORAL OBJECTIVES students will;

1. Take dictation using
2. Place the heart beats, bar lines and double bar line in a rhythm exercise.

MATERIALS; 1. TWO TERMINAL 4 WORKSHEETS AND PENCILS. 2. OVERHEAD AND TRANSPARENCIES FOR TERMINAL 4 WORKSHEETS.

PROCEDURE;

1. GREETING; sung as;   Hel-   lo   to   you.   (class echoes the same.)
                               s   1   s   m
                           ta   ta   ta   ta

2. OPENING SONG; "Teddy Bear." On this they will;
   a. Sing the words and clap the beat.
   b. Do some form of part work.

SPONGE ACTIVITY;

STATE OBJECTIVES;

3. DICTATION; Method of procedure.
   a. Distribute dictation worksheets.
   b. Place worksheets on overhead and point out heading. Review method of taking dictation. Write the rhythm signs when dictated under the side titled stems. When the dictation is ended go back and write the notes that correspond with the stems.
   c. Distribute pencils and give dictation.
(BEHAVIORAL OBJECTIVE 1)

4. RHYTHM WORKSHEET ACTIVITY; Method of procedure.
   a. Distribute terminal 4 rhythm worksheets.
   b. Place worksheets on over head and point out heading. Discuss procedure for filling out sheet.
   c. Distribute pencils. Students are to fill out the worksheets independently.

(BEHAVIORAL OBJECTIVE 2)

5. PLAY PARTIES; Several familiar ones.

6. GOOD-BYE; sung as;   Good- bye   to   you.   (class echoes the same.)
                                 s   1   s   m
                           ta   ta   ta   ta

WRITE ON BOARD; 1. TAKE DICTATION USING
  2. FILL IN A WORKSHEET.

NAME _____ CLASS _____ DATE _____

STEMS	NOTES

STEMS

NOTES

1._____

1._____

2._____

2._____

3._____

3._____

4._____

4._____

5._____

5._____

6._____

6._____

7._____

7._____

8._____

8._____

9._____

9._____

10._____

10._____

TERMINAL 4 WORKSHEET NO. ONE OF TWO.

NAME _____ CLASS _____ DATE _____

1. Write the heart beats.
2. Place the bar lines according to the top number of the time signature.
3. Do not forget the double bar line.

TERMINAL 4 WORKSHEET NO. TWO OF TWO.

56

LESSON 16
INSTRUCTIONAL OBJECTIVES;
1. PREPARE re.
2. PRESENT la on the staff.
3. PRACTICE writing s 1 m on the staff.

BEHAVIORAL OBJECTIVES; students will;
1. Learn a new song. (INSTRUCTIONAL OBJECTIVE 1)
2. Derive a generalization statement for la. (INSTRUCTIONAL OBJECTIVE 2)
3. Practice writing s l m patterns on the staff. (INSTRUCTIONAL OBJECTIVE 3)

MATERIALS; 1. SONG; "BUTTON YOU MUST WANDER." 2. BIG CHART FOR SLM.
3. FLANNEL BOARDS, PELON STAFFS, AND FELT CIRCLES. 4. FLASH CARDS.
5. MAGNETIC BOARD AND MAGNETIC DISCS.

PROCEDURE;
1. GREETING; sung as; Hel-   lo   to   you.   (class echoes the same.)
                         s   1   s   m

2. OPENING SONG; "Teddy Bear." On this they will;
    a. Sing the words and clap the beat.
    b. Do some form of part work.

3. FLASH CARD ACTIVITY; Select one or both.

___ a. Known rhythm cards.

___ b. Known solfege / rhythm cards.

STATE OBJECTIVES;

4. NEW SONG; "Button You Must Wander." On this they will;
    a. Learn the song by rote.
    b. Sing the words and clap the beat.
    c. Sing and clap the rhythm syllables.
    d. Use inner hearing to internalize the song.
(BEHAVIORAL OBJECTIVE 1)

5. PRESENT LA ON THE STAFF; Method of presentation;
    a. Teacher sings two s 1 m exercises from the big chart. One with so on a line.
        Another with so in the space.
    b. Leads a discussion about la in relationship to so.
    c. Class discovers that when so is on a line, la is in the space above it. When so is in
        a space la is on the line above it.
    d. Class reads both exercises.
(BEHAVIORAL OBJECTIVE 2)

6. WRITING ACTIVITY; Distribute flannel boards, pelon staffs, and felt circles. Rules are given for using this material.
    a. Class places the pelon staff on the flannel board.
    b. Class is told where to place so.
    c. Teacher sings a s 1 m pattern.
    d. Students place circles for pattern.
    e. Teacher places pattern on the magnetic board.
(BEHAVIORAL OBJECTIVE 3)

7. CLOSURE; 1. Name the new song learned today. 2. State the so la generalization statement.

8. GOOD-BYE; sung as; Good-   bye   to   you.   (class echoes the same.)
                         s   1   s   m

WRITE ON BOARD; 1. LEARN A NEW SONG. 2. PLACE LA ON THE STAFF. 3. WRITE S L M PATTERNS ON THE STAFF.

BUTTON YOU MUST WANDER

| 2 | d | d | d | r | m | s | r | s | m | d |
| 4 | But- | ton | you | must | wan- | der, | wan- | der, | wan- | der. |

| d | d | d | r | m | s | r | s | d |
| But- | ton | you | must | wan- | der, | ev'- | ry | where. |

| 1 | 1 | 1 | s | d | 1 | 1 | 1 | s | d |
| Bright | eyes | will | find | you. | Sharp | eyes | will | find | you. |

| d | d | d | r | m | s | r | s | d |
| But- | ton | you | must | wan- | der, | ev'- | ry | where. |

GAME; Formation - circle with one child in the center.
1. All sing the song and pass the button. The center child closes his or her eyes.
2. When the song ends all hands are closed in front position.
3. The center child tries to guess who has the button.
4. When the button is found that child becomes the center person.
5. After about three or four guesses if the button is not found, the child holding the button reveals it. This person becomes the center person and the game begins again.

LESSON 16 GRADE_____ TEACHER_____

TERMINAL 5 AFTER LESSON 16

BEHAVIORAL OBJECTIVES; students will;
1. Read the solfege and write six so la mi patterns on the staff.
2. Read the pitch and rhythm of an unfamiliar song. Copy the same song on the staff.

MATERIALS; 1. PENCILS AND STAFF PAPER. 2. TWO TERMINAL 5 WORKSHEETS.
(Teacher selects or makes these.) 3. OVERHEAD AND TRANSPARENCIES FOR TERMINAL
5 WORKSHEETS.

PROCEDURE;
1. GREETING; sung as; Hel-   lo   to   you.   (class echoes the same.)
                       s   1   s   m
                       ta   ta   ta   ta

2. OPENING SONG; "Button You Must Wander." On this they will;
   a. Sing the words and clap the beat.
   b. Do some form of part work.

SPONGE ACTIVITY;

STATE OBJECTIVES;

3. READING AND WRITING ACTIVITY;
   a. Terminal five worksheets are distributed.
   b. Teacher uses overhead to give instruction for filling in the worksheets. Teacher chooses
      method of presentation.
   c. Pencils are distributed and students fill in the worksheets independently.
(BEHAVIORAL OBJECTIVE 1 AND 2)

4. PLAY PARTIES; Several familiar ones.

5. GOOD-BYE; sung as; Good-   bye   to   you.   (class echoes the same.)
                      s   1   s   m

WRITE ON BOARD; 1. READ AND WRITE SIX SO LA MI PATTERNS ON THE STAFF.
2. READ AN UNFAMILIAR SONG ON THE STAFF.

TERMINAL 5   GRADE _____ TEACHER_____

SIX SO LA MI PATTERNS ON THE STAFF. Place so on the second line.

1.

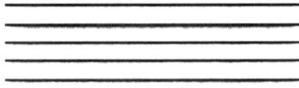

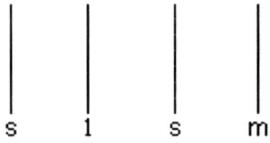

s   l   s   m

4.

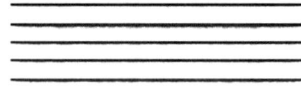

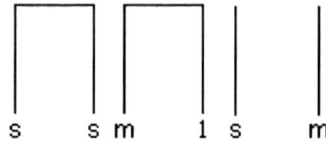

s   s m   l s   m

2.

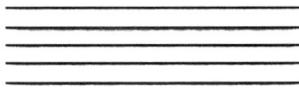

m   s   l   s

5.

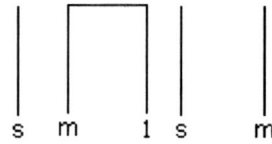

s m l s   m

3.

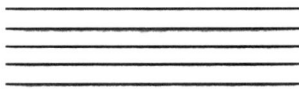

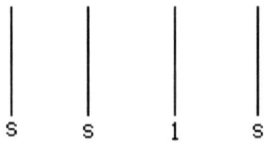

s   s   l   s

6.

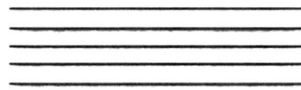

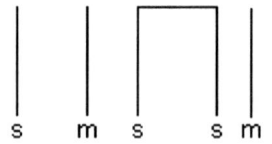

s m s s m

TERMINAL 5 WORKSHEET NO. ONE OF TWO.

LESSON 17
INSTRUCTIONAL OBJECTIVES;
1. PREPARE tiritiri.
2. PRESENT low do on the tone ladder.
3. PRACTICE singing on the tone ladder.

BEHAVIORAL OBJECTIVES; students will;
1. Learn a new song. (INSTRUCTIONAL OBJECTIVE 1)
2. Learn a new pitch syllable. (INSTRUCTIONAL OBJECTIVE 2)
3. Sing a familiar song on the tone ladder. (INSTRUCTIONAL OBJECTIVE 3)

MATERIALS; 1. SONG; "DINAH." 2. FLASH CARDS. 3. MAGNETIC HEART FOR PITCH CHART. 4. MAGNETIC DO FOR TONE LADDER.

PROCEDURE;
1. GREETING; sung as; Hel-   lo   to   you.   (class echoes the same.)
                         s   1   s   m

2. OPENING SONG; "Button You Must Wander." On this they will;
   a. Sing the words and clap the beat.
   b. Do some form of part work.

3. FLASH CARD ACTIVITY; Select one or both.

___ a. Known rhythm cards.

___ b. Known Solfege / rhythm cards

STATE OBJECTIVES;

4. NEW SONG; "Dinah." On this they will;
   a. Learn the song by rote.
   b. Clap the beat while singing the words.
   c. Clap the way the words go.
   d. Use inner hearing to internalize the song.
(BEHAVIORAL OBJECTIVE 1)

5. PRESENT LOW DO ON THE TONE LADDER; Presentation song "Ring Around the Rosie."
   a. Class sings song.
   b. Derives the rhythm by clapping and singing the rhythm syllables. Teacher writes the rhythm on the board.
   c. Follow directions for DERIVING MELODY OF A SONG WITH ONE UNKNOWN TONE.
   d. After the new tone is found, the hand sign is shown; do is placed on the tone ladder; a heart is placed on the pitch chart; and hand sign is turned over on hand sign ladder.
(BEHAVIORAL OBJECTIVE 2)

PAGE 2 LESSON 17

6. STUDENT PERFORMANCE; Known songs that may be used;
    a. Ring Around The Rosie.
    b. Peas Porridge.
    c. Fuzzy Wuzzy.

    Teacher draws a drm sl tone ladder on the board and demonstrates how to sing a song on the tone ladder. After a brief period of study, students are given the opportunity to come before the class and sing the same song on the tone ladder.
(BEHAVIORAL OBJECTIVE 3)

7. CLOSURE; 1. Name the new song learned today. 2. Name the new pitch learned today. 3. Give the hand sign for the new pitch learned today.

8. GOOD-BYE; sung as; Good-   bye   to   you.   *z*   (class echoes the same.)
                            s   m   m   d   —
                            ta   ti   ti   ta   —

WRITE ON BOARD; 1. LEARN A NEW SONG. 2. LEARN A NEW PITCH SYLLABLE. 3. SING A FAMILIAR SONG ON THE TONE LADDER.

DINAH

2
4   d d d d   d   m | s   m   s   m |
    No one in the house but | Di- nah, Di- nah. |

    d d d d   d   m | r   r   d |
    No one in the house but | me   I   know. |

    d d d d   d   m | s   m   s   m |
    No one in the house but | Di- nah, Di- nah. |

    r r r r   m   r | d ||
    Strum-ing on the old ban- | jo. ||

GAME; Circle formation with one child in the center blindfolded. Another child stand in the center behind the blindfolded child and is the only one who sings "Dinah, Dinah" each time it comes in the song. At the end of the song, the child who sings "Dinah, Dinah" goes back into the circle. The blindfolded child must guess who was singing.

LESSON 18
INSTRUCTIONAL OBJECTIVES;
1. PREPARE ti tiri.
2. PRESENT re on the tone ladder.
3. PRACTICE singing a song on the tone ladder.

BEHAVIORAL OBJECTIVE; students will;
1. Learn a new song. (INSTRUCTIONAL OBJECTIVE 1)
2. Learn a new pitch syllable. (INSTRUCTIONAL OBJECTIVE 2)
3. Sing a song on the tone ladder. (INSTRUCTIONAL OBJECTIVE 3)

MATERIALS; 1. SONG; "GREAT GRAND DAD." 2. BIG CHART. 3. MAGNETIC RE.
4. FLASH CARDS. 5. A BUTTON FOR THE GAME.

PROCEDURE;
1. GREETING; sung as; Hel-   lo   to   you.   z   (class echoes the same.)
                           s   m   m   d   —
                           ta   ti   ti   ta   —

2. 2, OPENING SONG; "Dinah." On this they will;
   a. Sing the words and clap the beat.
   b. Do some form of part work.

3. FLASH CARD ACTIVITY; Select one or both.

___ a. Known rhythm cards.

___ b. Known solfege / rhythm cards.

STATE OBJECTIVES;

4. NEW SONG; "Great Grand Dad." On this they will;
   a. Learn the song by rote.
   b. Clap the beat while singing the words.
   c. Clap the way the words go.
   d. Use inner hearing to internalize the song.
(BEHAVIORAL OBJECTIVE 1)

5. PRESENT RE ON THE TONE LADDER. Presentation song "Hot Cross Buns."
   a. Class sings song.
   b. Derives rhythm. Teacher or student writes rhythm on board.
   c. Follow directions for DERIVING MELODY OF A SONG WITH ONE UNKNOWN TONE.
   d. After the new tone has been found, re is placed on the tone ladder; a magnetic
      heart is placed beside re on the pitch sign; hand sign is turned over on the hand
      sign ladder.
(BEHAVIORAL OBJECTIVE 2)

6. SINGING ACTIVITY; Teacher selects a song. Sings the song on the tone ladder. Students are given the opportunity to do the same.
   Choices;
   a. Button You Must Wander
   b. Fuzzy Wuzzy
   c. Hot Cross Buns
   d. Bow Wow Wow
   e. Peas Porridge Hot
   f. Ring Around the Rosie
   g. Teddy Bear
   h. Who's That

(BEHAVIORAL OBJECTIVE 3)

7. PLAY PARTY; "Button You Must Wander." (NEW)

8. CLOSURE; 1. Name the new song learned today. 2. Tell something about the new pitch learned today.

9. GOOD-BYE; sung as; Good- bye to you. z   (class echoes the same.)
                           s m m d, —
                           ta ti ti ta —

WRITE ON BOARD; 1 LEARN A NEW SONG. 2 LEARN A NEW PITCH SYLLABLE. 3. SING A SONG ON THE TONE LADDER.

GREAT GRAND DAD

2
4

s	m	1	s	s		m	s	d	
Great	Grand-	dad	when	the		land	was	young.	

r	m	f	m	r		m	1	s	s	s
Barred	the	door	with	a		wag-	on	tongue.	For	the

m	s	s	s	s		1	1	s	f	f
times	was	rough	and	the		dan-	gers	great,	and	he

m	s	s	m		r	r	s	d
said	his	prayers	both		ear-	ly	and	late.

LESSON 19
INSTRUCTIONAL OBJECTIVES;
1. PREPARE the slur.
2. PRESENT (a) Low do on the staff. (b) The do clef. (c) Leger line.
3. PRACTICE reading s m d on the staff.

BEHAVIORAL OBJECTIVES; students will;
1. Learn a new song. (INSTRUCTIONAL OBJECTIVE 1)
2. Derive a generalization statement for low do. (INSTRUCTIONAL OBJECTIVE 2)
3. Learn the use of the do clef. (INSTRUCTIONAL OBJECTIVE 3)
4. Learn about the ledger line. (INSTRUCTIONAL OBJECTIVE 4)
5. Read a familiar song on the staff. (INSTRUCTIONAL OBJECTIVE 5)

MATERIAL; 1. SONG; "GREAT BIG HOUSE." 2. S M D, EXERCISE ON THE BIG CHART.
3. A BUTTON. 4. DO CLEF PICTURED ON UNIVERSAL BOARD.

PROCEDURE;
1. GREETING; sung as; Hel- lo   to   you. *z*   (class echoes the same.)
                        s   m   m   d   —
                        ta   ti   ti   ta   —

2. OPENING SONG; "Great Grand Dad." On this they will;
   a. Sing the words and clap the beat.
   b. Do some form of part work.

3. FLASH CARD ACTIVITY; Select one or both.

___ a. Known rhythm cards.

___ b. Known solfege / rhythm cards.

STATE OBJECTIVES;

4. NEW SONG; "Great Big House." On this they will;
   a. Learn the song by rote.
   b. Clap the beat while singing the words.
   c. Clap and sing the rhythm syllables.
   d. Use inner hearing to internalize the song.
(BEHAVIORAL OBJECTIVE 1)

5. PRESENT LOW DO ON THE STAFF; method of presentation; Teacher sings a s m d,
   exercise on the big chart. Leads a discussion about low do in relationship to so on the
   staff. Generalization statement is derived.
(BEHAVIORAL OBJECTIVE 2)

6. PRESENT THE DO CLEF; the symbol is shown and explained as the clef that locates do
   on the staff.
(BEHAVIORAL OBJECTIVE 3)

7. PRESENT THE LEGER LINE. An added line below or above the staff.
(BEHAVIORAL OBJECTIVE 4)

8. READING ACTIVITY; Teacher writes "Fuzzy Wuzzy" on the staff. Demonstrates how to
read the notes. Students are given the opportunity to do the same.
(BEHAVIORAL OBJECTIVE 5)

9. CHANGE OF PACE; "BUTTON YOU MUST WANDER" PLAY PARTY.

10. CLOSURE; 1. Name the new song learned today. 2. State the generalization statement
for do. What is the do clef used for?

11. GOOD-BYE; sung as; Good-   bye   to   you.   z   (class echoes the same.)
                                           s   m   m   d,   —
                                           ta   ti   ti   ta   —

WRITE ON BOARD; 1. LEARN A NEW SONG. 2. PLACE LOW DO ON THE STAFF.
3. LEARN ABOUT THE DO CLEF. 4 READ A FAMILIAR SONG ON THE STAFF.

GREAT BIG HOUSE IN NEW ORLEANS

2. Went down to the old mill stream
to fetch a pail of water.
Put one arm around my wife,
the other round my daughter.

3. Fare thee well my darling girl,
Fare thee well my daughter.
Fare thee well my darling girl
with the golden slippers on her.

LESSON 19 GRADE_____ TEACHER_____

LESSON 20

INSTRUCTIONAL OBJECTIVES;
1. PREPARE low la and low so.
2. PRESENT four sixteenth notes and the sixteenth rest.
3. PRACTICE reading beat with rhythm.

BEHAVIORAL OBJECTIVES; students will;
1. Learn a new song. (INSTRUCTIONAL OBJECTIVE 1)
2. Learn two new rhythm signs. (INSTRUCTIONAL OBJECTIVE 2)
3. Sing the rhythm and point to the beat of a familiar song. (INSTRUCTIONAL OBJECTIVE 3)

MATERIALS; 1. SONG; "ALABAMA GAL." 2. FOUR SIXTEENTH NOTES AND A SIXTEENTH REST ON THE RHYTHM DISPLAY AREA.

PROCEDURE;
1. GREETING; sung as; Hel- lo   to   you.   (class echoes the same.)
                        s   s   s   d
                        ta   ti   ti   too-oo

2. OPENING SONG; "Great Big House in New Orleans." On this they will;
    a. Sing the words and clap the beat.
    b. Do some form of part work.

3. FLASH CARD ACTIVITY; select one or both.

___ a. Known rhythm cards.

___ b. Known solfege / rhythm cards.

STATE OBJECTIVES;

4. NEW SONG; "Alabama Gal." On this they will;
    a. Learn a song by rote.
    b. Clap the beat and sing the words.
    c. Clap the way the words go.
    d. Use inner hearing to internalize the song.
(BEHAVIORAL OBJECTIVE 1)

5. PRESENT FOUR SIXTEENTH NOTES AND THE SIXTEENTH REST;
    Presentation song "Dinah."
    a. Class sings song.
    b. Teacher sings "no one in the" and claps 1 beat.
    c. Teacher asks the following: (q) How many sounds did you hear? (a) four. (q) How many beats did you hear? (a) one.
    d. Students are given time to find the new rhythm sign in the rhythm display area.
    e. After the sign is found, the note type is given as four sixteenth notes. The rhythm syllable is spoken as tiritiri and the hand clap is shown.

70

f. Teacher draws a single sixteenth note on the board telling the class that a sixteenth note can look two ways. Then draws a sixteenth rest and compares the stem and flags of each. The stem notation sign is drawn.
(BEHAVIORAL OBJECTIVE 2)

6. STUDENT PERFORMANCE OF RHYTHM WITH BEAT. Presentation song "Dinah."
    a. Teacher sings the rhythm of the song.
    b. Teacher and class sing the rhythm of the song.
    c. Teacher writes rhythm on board.
    d. A student is assigned to write the beat and tell why that beat is placed there. (ex. one sound for one beat.)
    e. Teacher models pointing to the beat and singing the rhythm. Students are given an opportunity to do the same.
(BEHAVIORAL OBJECTIVE 3)

7. CLOSURE; 1. Name the new song learned today. 2. Name the two rhythm signs learned today.

8. GOOD-BYE; sung as; Good- bye   to   you.   (class echoes the same.)
                        s   s   s   d
                        ta   ti   ti   too-oo

WRITE ON BOARD; 1. LEARN A NEW SONG. 2. LEARN TWO NEW RHYTHM SIGNS. 3. SING THE RHYTHM AND POINT TO THE BEAT OF A FAMILIAR SONG.

ALABAMA GAL

```
2  d     d     1,    d     m  |  d     d        d     1,    s,
4  You   don't  know  how,  how.  You   don't     know  how,  how.

   d     d     1,    d     m  |  m     s     m     r     d.
   You   don't  know  how,  how.  Al-   a-    bam-  a     gal.
```

2. I'll show you how, how. (3 times) Alabama gal.
3. Ain't I rock candy (3 times) Alabama gal.
4. Come through in a hurry. (3 times) Alabama gal.

LESSON 20 GRADE_____ TEACHER_____

TERMINAL 6 AFTER LESSON 20

BEHAVIORAL OBJECTIVES; students will;
1. Place beats and bar lines on a rhythm exercise using

MATERIALS; 1. PENCILS AND TERMINAL 6 WORKSHEETS. 2. FLASH CARDS.

PROCEDURE;

2. GREETING; sung as; Hel-   lo   to   you.   (new) (class echoes the same.)
                        s   m   m   d
                        ta   ti   ti   too-oo

3. OPENING SONG; "Alabama Gal." On this they will;
   a. Sing the words, sing the rhythm, and clap the beat on each.
   b. Do some form of part work.

SPONGE ACTIVITY;

STATE OBJECTIVES;

4. WORKSHEET ACTIVITY; Pencils and worksheets are passed out. Class reads
   instructions together then fill in the worksheets independently.
(BEHAVIORAL OBJECTIVE 1)

5. PLAY PARTY; Dinah. (new)

6. GOOD-BYE; sung as; Good-   bye   to   you.   (class echoes the same.)
                        s   m   m   d
                        ta   ti   ti   too-oo

WRITE ON BOARD; 1. PLACE BEATS AND BAR LINES ON A RHYTHM EXERCISE.

TERMINAL 6   GRADE _____ TEACHER_____

NAME _____ CLASS _____ DATE _____

1. Circle the top number of the time signature.
2. Place heart beats, bar lines and the double bar.

TERMINAL 6 WORKSHEET NO. ONE OF ONE.

LESSON 21
INSTRUCTIONAL OBJECTIVES;
1. PREPARE the slur.
2. PRESENT re on the staff.
3. PRACTICE writing a familiar song on the staff.

BEHAVIORAL OBJECTIVES; students will;
1. Learn a new song. (INSTRUCTIONAL OBJECTIVE 1)
2. Derive a generalization statement for re. (INSTRUCTIONAL OBJECTIVE 2)
3. Write a familiar song on the staff. (INSTRUCTIONAL OBJECTIVE 3)

MATERIALS; 1. SONG "LET US CHASE THE SQUIRREL." 2. FLASH CARDS. 3. BIG CHART.

PROCEDURE;
1. GREETING; sung as;   Hel-   lo   to   you.   *z*   (class echoes the same.)
                           s   m   m   d,   —
                           ta   ti   ti   ta   —

2. OPENING SONG; "Alabama Gal." On this they will;
    a. Sing the words and clap the beat.
    b. Do some form of part work.

3. FLASH CARD ACTIVITY; Select one or both
____ a. Known rhythm cards.

____ b. Known solfege / rhythm cards.

STATE OBJECTIVES;

4. NEW SONG; "Let Us Chase the Squirrel." On this they will;
    a. Learn the song by rote.
    b. Clap the beat while singing the words.
    c. Clap and sing the rhythm syllables.
    d. Use inner hearing to internalize the song.
(BEHAVIORAL OBJECTIVE 1)

5. PRESENT RE ON THE STAFF; method of presentation; The teacher sings a m r d,
    exercise on the big chart. Leads a discussion about re in relationship to do and mi.
    Generalization statement is derived. (Remind students that re is the passing tone
    between do and mi.)
(BEHAVIORAL OBJECTIVE 2)

6. WRITING ON THE STAFF; Presentation song "Hot Cross Buns."
    a. Class sings song.
    b. Derives rhythm by clapping and singing the rhythm syllables. Teacher writes this
        on the board.
    c. Class uses d, r m tone ladder to derive the melody.

   d. Teacher gives instruction for writing the song on the staff. Refer to the staff as a tone ladder. Bring out the fact that the steps on the staff move as line space. Teacher writes the song on the staff. Erases it.
   e. Students are given an opportunity to come to the board and write the song on the staff.

(BEHAVIORAL OBJECTIVE 3)

7. PLAY PARTY; "Dinah."

8. CLOSURE; 1. Name the new song learned today. 2. State the generalization statement for re.

9. GOOD-BYE; sung as;

Good-	bye	to	you.	(class echoes the same.)
	s	m	m	d,
	ta	ti	ti	too-oo

WRITE ON BOARD; 1. LEARN A NEW SONG. 2. PLACE RE ON THE STAFF. 3. WRITE A FAMILIAR SONG ON THE STAFF.

LET US CHASE THE SQUIRREL

| 2 | d | d | r | r | m_____s | d | d | r | r | m | m | r | r |
| 4 | Let | us | chase | the | squirrel | up | the | hick- | 'ry | down | the | hick- | 'ry |

d	d	r	r	m_____s	d	d	r	r	d
Let	us	chase	the	squirrel	up	the	hick-	'ry	tree.

   2. If you want to catch us, up the hick-ry down the hick-ry.
      If you want to catch us, learn to climb a tree.

PLAY PARTY; FORMATION; class separates in groups of three. They will decide who will be the one in the hole. The other two are the tree. They face each other and join hands to make a hole. The squirrel gets into the hole. Another child is the robber squirrel. The class sings both verses of the song while the robber squirrel skips around through the forest. On the word "tree" joined hands go up. The squirrels escape to find another hole. When the squirrel finds a new hole joined hands come down. The robber squirrel finds a hole and leaves a squirrel out of the hole. This is the new robber squirrel. The game begins again.

LESSON 21 GRADE_____ TEACHER_____

TERMINAL 7 AFTER LESSON 21
BEHAVIORAL OBJECTIVES; students will;
1. Write a familiar song on the staff.
2. Write an original eighth measure composition using do, re, mi, so, la and rhythm signs.

MATERIALS; 1. TWO TERMINAL 7 WORKSHEETS AND PENCILS. (Teacher selects or makes these.) 2 OVERHEAD AND TRANSPARENCIES OF TERMINAL 7 WORKSHEETS.

PROCEDURE;
1. GREETING; sung as; Hel- lo to you. (class echoes the same.)
           s   m   m   d
           ta   ti   ti   too-oo

2. OPENING SONG; "Let Us Chase The Squirrel." On this they will;
   a. Sing the words, sing the rhythm, and clap the beat on each.
   b. Do some form of part work.

SPONGE ACTIVITY;

STATE OBJECTIVES;

3. WRITING ACTIVITY;
   a. Teacher uses overhead and gives instruction for writing a familiar song on the staff and for writing an original composition. "Hot Cross Buns" worksheets are distributed.
   b. Pencils are distributed and students fill in the worksheet individually.
(BEHAVIORAL OBJECTIVE 1 AND 2)

4. PLAY PARTIES; Several familiar ones.

5. GOOD-BYE; sung as; Good- bye to you. (class echoes the same.)
           s   m   m   d
           ta   ti   ti   too-oo

WRITE ON BOARD; 1. WRITE A FAMILIAR SONG ON THE STAFF. 2. WRITE AN ORIGINAL EIGHT MEASURE COMPOSITION USING DO, RE, MI, SO, LA PITCH SYLLABLES AND RHYTHM SIGNS.

TERMINAL 7   GRADE _____ TEACHER_____

NAME _____ CLASS _____ DATE _____

Write "Hot Cross Buns" on the staff.

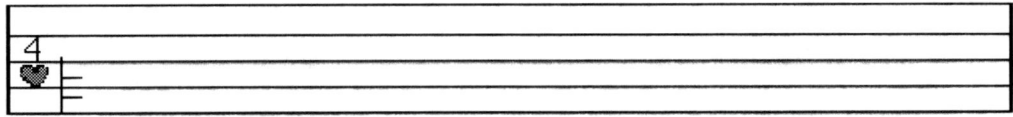

| | |
m   r   d   _

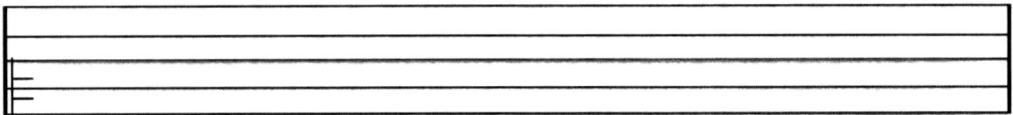

| | |
m   r   d   _

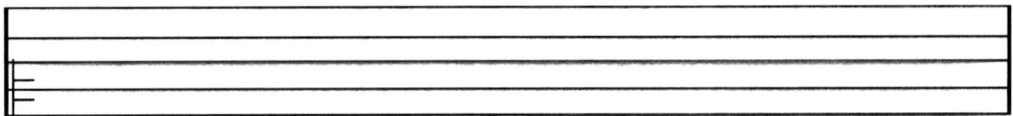

d   d   d   d   r   r   r   r

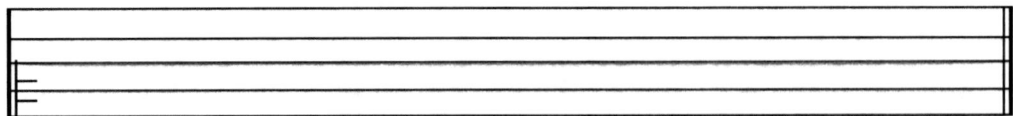

| | |
m   r   d   _

TERMINAL 7 WORKSHEET NO. ONE OF TWO.

NAME _____ CLASS _____ DATE _____

WRITE AN ORIGINAL COMPOSITION;
1. Circle the top number of the time signature.
2. Write a letter under the staff for each note. Use one dash for the quarter rest and two dashes for the half rest.
3. Place the heart beats. Check the time signature for the number of beats in each measure.

TONE ROW

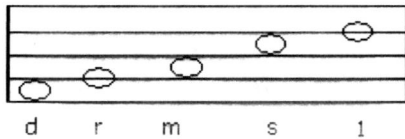

d   r   m   s   l

RHYTHM SIGNS

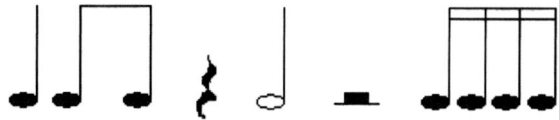

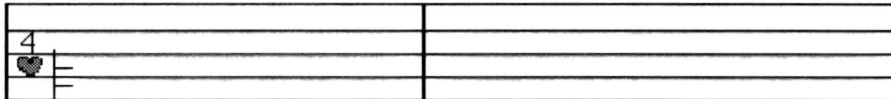

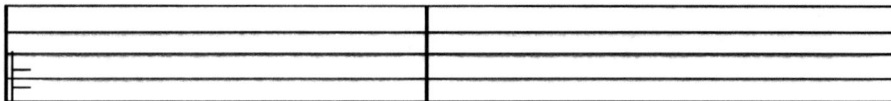

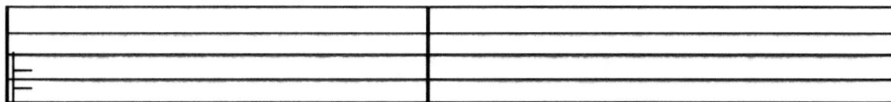

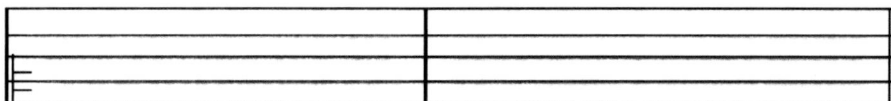

TERMINAL 7 WORKSHEET NO. TWO OF TWO.

LESSON 22
INSTRUCTIONAL OBJECTIVES;
1. PRESENT (a) Tone color. (b) Instruments of the orchestra.
2. PRACTICE distinguishing tone color.

BEHAVIORAL OBJECTIVES; students will;
1. Learn a new song.
2. Learn the meaning of the tone color. (INSTRUCTIONAL OBJECTIVE 1)
3. Learn the names of the four families of instruments in the orchestra.
    (INSTRUCTIONAL OBJECTIVE 2)
4. Aurally distinguish tone color of instruments and voices.
    (INSTRUCTIONAL OBJECTIVE 3)

MATERIALS; 1. SONG; "DOGGIE, DOGGIE." 2. TEACHER SELECTED MATERIAL ON
INSTRUMENTS OF THE ORCHESTRA. 3. FLASH CARDS. 4. CLASS ROOM INSTRUMENTS.

PROCEDURE;
1. GREETING; sung as; Hel-   lo   to   you.   z   (class echoes the same.)
                         m   r   r   d,   —
                         ta   ti   ti   ta   —

2. OPENING SONG; "Let Us Chase The Squirrel." On this they will;
    a. Sing the words and clap the beat.
    b. Do some form of part work.

3. FLASH CARD ACTIVITY; Select one or both.

___ a. Known rhythm cards.

___ b. Known solfege / rhythm cards.

STATE OBJECTIVES;

4. NEW SONG; "Doggie, Doggie." On this they will;
    a. Learn the song by rote.
    b. Sing the words and clap the beat.
    c. Sing and clap the rhythm syllables.
    d. Use inner hearing to internalize the song.
(BEHAVIORAL OBJECTIVE 1)

5. PRESENT TONE COLOR; Method of presentation;
    a. Define tone color.
    b. Teacher uses selected materials and makes class conscious of family names of
        instruments only.
(BEHAVIORAL OBJECTIVE 2)

6. CHANGE OF PACE - VOICE AND INSTRUMENT RECOGNITION;
   Presentation song "Doggie, Doggie."
   a. Class sings song.
   b. Students put their heads on the desk and sing the song.
   c. The teacher touches someone and they sing "I STOLE THE BONE."
   d. Students will identify the person singing the answer.
   e. Teacher plays an instrument hiding it so the students cannot see it. Students are
      to identify the instrument.
   (BEHAVIORAL OBJECTIVE 3)

7. PLAY PARTY; "Let Us Chase The Squirrel." (NEW)

8. CLOSURE; 1. Name the new song learned today. 2. Review names of families of
   instruments.

9. GOOD-BYE; sung as; Good- bye   to   you.   *z*   (class echoes the same.)
                         s   m   m   d,   —
                         ta   ti   ti   ta   —

WRITE ON BOARD; 1. LEARN A NEW SONG. 2. LEARN THE NAMES OF THE FOUR
FAMILIES OF INSTRUMENTS IN THE SYMPHONY ORCHESTRA.

DOGGIE, DOGGIE

$\frac{2}{4}$

s   s   m   m   s   s   m
Dog- gie, Dog- gie   where's your bone?

s   s   m   1   s   s   m
Some- one stole it   from   my   home!

s   m   1   s   m
Who stole the   bone?_____

s   m   1   s   m
I   stole the   bone?_____

LESSON 23
INSTRUCTIONAL OBJECTIVES;
1. PRESENT families of instruments.
2. PRACTICE in tune singing.

BEHAVIORAL OBJECTIVES; students will;
1. Learn a new song. (INSTRUCTIONAL OBJECTIVE 1)
2. Place instruments in families. (INSTRUCTIONAL OBJECTIVE 2)
3. Sing and play "Fuzzy Wuzzy." (INSTRUCTIONAL OBJECTIVE 3)

MATERIALS; 1. SONG; "ROCKY MOUNTAIN." 2. TEACHER SELECTED MATERIALS FOR INSTRUMENTS OF THE ORCHESTRA. 3. BIG XYLOPHONE. 4. INSTRUMENT NAMES ON MAGNETIC CARDS. 5. A MAGNETIC BOARD FOR EACH FAMILY. 6. FLASH CARDS.

PROCEDURE;
1. GREETING; sung as; Hel-   lo   to   you.   (class echoes the same.)
                       s   m   m   d,
                       ta   ti   ti   too-oo

2. OPENING SONG; "Doggie, Doggie." On this they will;
   a. Sing the words and clap the beat.
   b. Do some form of part work.

3. FLASH CARD ACTIVITY; Select one or both.

___ a. Known rhythm cards.

___ b. Known solfege / rhythm cards.

STATE OBJECTIVES;

4. NEW SONG; "Rocky Mountain." On this they will;
   a. Learn the song by rote.
   b. Clap the beat and sing the words.
   c. Sing and clap the rhythm syllables.
   d. Use inner hearing to internalize the song.
(BEHAVIORAL OBJECTIVE 1)

5. PRESENT INSTRUMENTS IN FAMILIES;
   Teacher chooses method of presentation.
(BEHAVIORAL OBJECTIVE 2)

6. CLOSURE; 1. Name the new song learned today. 2. Pass out instrument names.
   Students will place their card in the correct family on the magnetic boards.

82

7. MUSIC PERFORMANCE. Students will sing "Fuzzy Wuzzy" and play an ostinato pattern on the xylophone.
   a. Teacher models what the students are to do.
   b. Students are given an opportunity to do the same performance.
(BEHAVIORAL OBJECTIVE 3)
8. GOOD-BYE; sung as; Good- bye   to   you.   (class echoes the same.)
                        s   m   m   d,
                        ta   ti   ti   too-oo

WRITE ON BOARD; 1. LEARN A NEW SONG. 2. PLACE INSTRUMENTS IN FAMILIES. 3. SING FUZZY WUZZY AND PLAY AND OSTINATO ON THE XYLOPHONE.

ROCKY MOUNTAIN

2. Sunny valley, sunny valley, sunny valley low.
    When you're in that sunny valley, sing it soft and slow.
    Do, do, do, do, do remember me.
    Do, do, do, do, do remember me.

3. Stormy ocean, stormy ocean, stormy ocean wide.
    When you're on that deep blue sea there's no place you can hide.
    Do, do, do, do, do remember me.
    Do, do, do, do, do remember me.

LESSON 23 GRADE_____ TEACHER_____

LESSON 24
INSTRUCTIONAL OBJECTIVES;
1. PREPARE syn co pa rhythm.
2. PRACTICE listening to families of instruments in the orchestra.

BEHAVIORAL OBJECTIVES; students will;
1. Learn a new song. (INSTRUCTIONAL OBJECTIVE 1)
2. Listen to families of instruments in the orchestra. (INSTRUCTIONAL OBJECTIVE 2)

MATERIALS; 1. SONG; "WEAVILY WHEAT." 2. TEACHER SELECTED MATERIALS ON
FAMILIES OF INSTRUMENTS AND RELATED WORKSHEET. 3. FLASH CARDS.

PROCEDURE;
1. GREETINGS; sung as; Hel-   lo   to   you.   (class echoes the same.)
                          s   s   s   d,
                          ta   ti   ti   too-oo

2. OPENING SONG; "Rocky Mountain." On this they will;
    a. Sing the words and clap the beat.
    b. Do some form or part work.

3. FLASH CARD ACTIVITY; Select one or both.

___ a. Known rhythm cards.

___ b. Known solfege / rhythm cards.

STATE OBJECTIVES;

4. NEW SONG; "Weavily Wheat." On this they will;
    a. Learn the song by rote.
    b. Tap the beat and sing the words.
    c. Clap the way the words go.
    d. Use inner hearing to internalize the song.
(BEHAVIORAL OBJECTIVE 1)

5. REVIEW INSTRUMENTS OF THE ORCHESTRA;
    Teacher selects method of presentation.
(BEHAVIORAL OBJECTIVE 2)

6. CLOSURE; 1. Name the new song learned today. 2. Students review teacher made or
    selected worksheet. 3. Students are reminded that they will take this in the next class
    session.

7. GOOD-BYE; sung as; Good-   bye   to   you.   (class echoes the same.)
                          s   s   s   d,
                          ta   ti   ti   too-oo

84

PAGE 2 LESSON 24

WRITE ON BOARD; 1. LEARN A NEW SONG. 2. LISTEN TO FAMILIES OF INSTRUMENTS IN THE ORCHESTRA.

WEAVILY WHEAT

2/4	m	d	s,	1, s, 1, s,	m	d	m	s	s
	Don't	want	your	weav-ily wheat,	don't	want	your	bar-	ley.

1	s	m	d	r	d	1,	1,	s,	s,	m	r	d	d
Take	some	flour	in	half	an	hour	and	bake	a	cake	for	Char-	lie.

m	m	d	d	1,	1,	s,	m	m	d	m	s	s
Five	times	five	is	twen-	ty	five,	five	times	six	is	thir-	ty.

1	s	m	d	r	d	1,	s,	s,	m	r	d	d
Five	times	sev'n	is	thir-	ty	five,	five	times	eight	is	for-	ty.

SECOND PART OF TIME TABLES.
Five times nine is forty five.
Five times ten is fifty.
Five times eleven is fifty five
Five times twelve is sixty. (END WITH FIRST TWO LINES)

GAME; FORMATION; Players stand in squares of four. Place right hand palm (fingers up) on the person's palm across from you. Two people's palms up and the other two palms under them. All sing song and walk in a circle keeping palms in place. On the time tables, all players bring hands to their side and stand in place. One at a time, layer left hands on atop the other each time the number is sung. All hands go up on the last word and the game starts again.

LESSON 24 GRADE_____ TEACHER_____

85

LESSON 25
INSTRUCTIONAL OBJECTIVES;
1. PREPARE ti-tiri.
2. PRESENT the slur.
3. PRACTICE test taking skills.

BEHAVIORAL OBJECTIVES; students will;
1. Learn a new song. (INSTRUCTIONAL OBJECTIVE 1)
2. Learn a new music sign. (INSTRUCTIONAL OBJECTIVE 2)
3. Place instruments in correct family. (INSTRUCTIONAL OBJECTIVE 3)

MATERIALS; 1. SONG; "KOOKABURRA." 2. SLUR SIGN ON UNIVERSAL LANGUAGE
BOARD. 3. PENCILS AND THE FAMILY OF INSTRUMENTS WORKSHEETS. 5. FLASH
CARDS.

PROCEDURE;
1. GREETINGS; sung as; Hel-   lo   to   you.   (class echoes the same.)
                         s   s   s   d,
                         ta   ti   ti   too-oo

2. OPENING SONG; "Weavily Wheat." On this they will;
    a. Sing the words and clap the beat.
    b. Do some form of part work.

3. FLASH CARD ACTIVITY; Select one or both.

____ a. Known rhythm cards.

____ b. Known solfege / rhythm cards.

STATE OBJECTIVES;

4. NEW SONG; "Kookaburra." On this they will;
    a. Learn the song by rote.
    b. Tap the beat and sing the words.
    c. Clap the way the words go.
    d. Use inner hearing to internalize the song.
(BEHAVIORAL OBJECTIVE 1)

5. PRESENT THE SLUR AS A MUSIC SIGN THAT IS A CURVE LINE OVER TWO OR MORE
    DIFFERENT NOTES SUNG ON ONE WORD.
    Presentation song "Great Big House."
    a. Class sings song
    b. Teacher sings the word, "high."
    c. (q) How many tones did you hear on that word? (ans.) two.
    d. There is a music sign that tells us to sing two or more different tones on one word.
        Can someone find this sign on the Universal Language Board? (Gives students
        time to find sign.)

e. When sign is found, teacher places the word "high" on the board with a line after it. One ta sign over the word and another ta sign placed after the word in a low position. Place a slur over the ta signs.
f. Class sings "high" observing the slur sign.
g. Teacher may want to include the slur as part of the songs that were used to prepare the slur.
(BEHAVIORAL OBJECTIVE 2)

6. INSTRUMENT WORKSHEET. Distribute worksheets and pencils. Students are instructed to read directions and fill in the worksheets.
(BEHAVIORAL OBJECTIVE 3)

7. PLAY PARTY; WEAVILY WHEAT. (NEW)

8. CLOSURE; 1. Name the new song learned today. 2. Review what a slur is.

7. GOOD-BYE; sung as; Good_____ bye._____   (class echoes the same.)
                       s   m   s   m
(Slur each syllable of the word.)

WRITE ON BOARD; 1. LEARN A NEW SONG. 2 LEARN A NEW MUSIC SIGN. 3. REVIEW INSTRUMENTS OF THE ORCHESTRA.

KOOKABURRA

2	s s s	s	1 1 1	s	m	s m
4	Kook-a-bur-ra	sits	on the	old	gum	tree._____

m m m m	f f f	m	d	m d
Mer-ry, mer-ry	king of the	bush	is	he._____

d'	1 t d' 1	s	s 1 s f
Laugh,	Kook-a-bur-ra,	laugh,	Kook-a-bur-ra

m	d	d	d	d
gay	your	life	must	be.

SOME SUGGESTED MATERIALS FOR THIS LESSON;
1. Young People's Guide to the Orchestra
2. Meet Big Bird's Orchestra.
3. Peter and the Wolf
4. Instrument Bingo

LESSON 25 GRADE_____ TEACHER_____

LESSON 26
INSTRUCTIONAL OBJECTIVES;
1. PREPARE triola.
2. PRESENT form.

BEHAVIORAL OBJECTIVES; students will;
1. Learn a new song. (INSTRUCTIONAL OBJECTIVE 1)
2. Visually identify form through the use of notational devices.
   (INSTRUCTIONAL OBJECTIVE 2)

MATERIALS; 1. SONG; "SALLY GO ROUND THE SUN." 2. FLASH CARDS.

PROCEDURE;
1. GREETINGS; sung as; Hel_____ lo._____   (class echoes the same.)
                         s   m   s   m   (slur each syllable of the
                                                         word.)

2. OPENING SONG; "Kookaburra." On this they will;
   a. Sing the words and clap the beat.
   b. Do some form of part work.

3. FLASH CARD ACTIVITY; Select one or both.

___ a. Known rhythm cards.

___ b. Known solfege / rhythm cards.

STATE OBJECTIVES;

4. NEW SONG; "Sally Go Round the Sun." On this they will;
   a. Learn the song by rote.
   b. Tap the beat while singing the words.
   c. Clap the way the words go.
   d. Use inner hearing to internalize the song.
(BEHAVIORAL OBJECTIVE 1)

5. PRESENT FORM AS THE FORMAT OF A SONG. Presentation song "Bow, Wow, Wow."
   a. Class sings song.
   b. Derives the rhythm by singing the rhythm syllables.
   c. Teacher writes the rhythm on the board four lines one measure each.
   d. Form is explained as two or more contrasting patterns in one song.
   e. Students are guided into identifying the form of the rhythm for "Bow, Wow, Wow."
(BEHAVIORAL OBJECTIVE 2)

6. PLAY PARTY; WEAVILY WHEAT (NEW)

7. CLOSURE; 1. Name the new song learned today. 2. Review the definition of form.
   3. Do a word drill that involves contrast. Example; teacher says "up", student says "down", etc.

8. GOOD-BYE; sung as; Good_____ bye._____   (class echoes the same.)
                           s   m   s   m   (slur each syllable of the word.)

WRITE ON BOARD; 1. LEARN A NEW SONG. 2. LEARN A NEW MUSIC ELEMENT.

SALLY GO ROUND THE SUN

PLAY PARTY; Class forms a double circle facing opposite directions. Class sings the song and moves to the beat in opposite directions. On the word "noon", each circle turns and moves the opposite direction.

ANOTHER WAY; Class forms a double circle facing same direction. Outside circle starts singing and stepping to the beat. At a designated point, the inside circle starts at the beginning of the song singing and stepping to the beat. The outside circle continues, ends first, stands still until the inside circle has finished.

LESSON 26 GRADE_____ TEACHER_____

LESSON 27
INSTRUCTIONAL OBJECTIVES;
1. PREPARE low so.
2. PRACTICE (a) Deriving the rhythm and form of a familiar song. (b) Derive the form of a musical selection.

BEHAVIORAL OBJECTIVES; students will;
1. Learn a new song. (INSTRUCTIONAL OBJECTIVE 1)
2. Derive the rhythm and form of a familiar song (INSTRUCTIONAL OBJECTIVE 2)
3. Aurally identify the form of a musical selection. (INSTRUCTIONAL OBJECTIVE 3)

MATERIALS; 1. SONG; "JOHN KANAKA." 2. TEACHER SELECTED MATERIALS ON LISTENING FOR FORM.

PROCEDURE;
1. GREETINGS; sung as; Hel-   lo   to   you.____   (class echoes the same.)
                             s   m   1   s   m   (slur "you.")
                             ta   ti   ti   ta   ta

2. OPENING SONG; "Sally Go Round The Sun." On this they will;
    a. Sing the words and clap the beat.
    b. Do some form of part work.

3. FLASH CARD ACTIVITY; Select one or both.

____ a. Known rhythm cards.

____ b. Known solfege / rhythm cards.

STATE OBJECTIVES;

4. NEW SONG; "John Kanaka." On this they will;
    a. Learn the song by rote.
    b. Clap the beat and sing the words.
    c. Clap the way the words go.
    d. Use inner hearing to internalize the song.
(BEHAVIORAL OBJECTIVE 1)

5. DERIVE RHYTHM AND FORM; PRESENTATION SONG "BOW, WOW, WOW."
    a. Class sings song.
    b. Derives rhythm. Teacher or student writes rhythm on board. (Four lines four beats each.)
    c. Students are given an opportunity to identify the form.
(BEHAVIORAL OBJECTIVE 2)

6. LISTENING ACTIVITY; Teacher selects method of presentation.
(BEHAVIORAL OBJECTIVE 3)

PAGE 2 LESSON 27

7. PLAY PARTY; "Sally Go Round The Sun." (NEW)

8. CLOSURE; 1. Name the new song learned today. 2. Define form. 3. State the name of the selection that was listened to and what was the form.

9. GOOD-BYE; sung as; Good-   bye   to   you._____   (class echoes the same.)
                              s   m   1   s   m   (slur "you.")
                              ta   ti   ti   ta   ta

WRITE ON BOARD; 1. LEARN A NEW SONG. 2. DERIVE RHYTHM AND FORM OF A FAMILIAR SONG. 3. DERIVE THE FORM OF A MUSICAL SELECTION.

JOHN KANAKA

2/4

m s   m s   m d r m
I heard   I heard the old man say.

d. r m m m m r s, d
John Ka- na- ka- na- ka too- lee- aye.

m s m s s m d r m
To- day, to- day is a hol- i- day.

d r m m m m r s, d
John Ka- na- ka- na- ka too- lee- aye.

s m s   s m s
Too- lee- aye.   Too- lee- aye.

d r m m m m r s, d
John Ka- na- ka- na- ka too- lee- aye.

PLAY PARTY;
1. Children form an outside circle and an inside circle.
2. Circles face each other and establish partners.
3. On the words "I heard, I heard," do si do with partner.
4. On "John" stamp foot.
   On "Kanaka naka" tap knees in rhythm.
   On "Toolee" clap own hands twice.
   On "aye" clap partner's hands once.
5. On "today, today" repeat do si do with partner.
6. Repeat step 4.
7. On the "aye" of the next two tooleeayes, outside circle step left and inside circle step right to establish a new partner.
8. Repeat step 4. Games begins again with a new partner.

LESSON 27 GRADE_____ TEACHER_____

LESSON 28

INSTRUCTIONAL OBJECTIVES;
1. PREPARE (a) 6/8 time. (b) low so and low la.
2. PRESENT ti tiri.
3. PRACTICE writing a rhythm composition in ABACA form.

BEHAVIORAL OBJECTIVES; students will;
1. Learn a new song. (INSTRUCTIONAL OBJECTIVE 1)
2. Learn a new rhythm sign and its syllable. (INSTRUCTIONAL OBJECTIVES 2)
3. Derive the rhythm and form of a familiar song. (INSTRUCTIONAL OBJECTIVES 3)
4. Write an ABACA rhythm pattern. (INSTRUCTIONAL OBJECTIVE 4)

MATERIALS; 1. SONG; "CHICKA MA". 2. FLASH CARDS.

PROCEDURE;
1. GREETINGS; sung as; Hel- lo   to   you.   (class echoes the same.)
                         s   m   m   d,
                         ta   ti   ti   too-oo

2. OPENING SONG; "John Kanaka." On this they will;
   a. Sing the words and clap the beat.
   b. Do some form of part work.

3. FLASH CARD ACTIVITY; Select one or the other.

___ a. Known rhythm cards.

___ b. Known solfege / rhythm cards.

STATE OBJECTIVES;

4. NEW SONG; "Chicka Ma." On this they will;
   a. Learn the song by rote.
   b. Clap the way the words go.
   c. Clap the beat and sing the words.
   d. Use inner hearing to internalize the song.
(BEHAVIORAL OBJECTIVE 1)

5. PRESENT TI TIRI; Presentation song "Kookaburra."
   a. Class sings song.
   b. Teacher targets "sits on the." (q) How many sounds did you hear? (a) Three. (q) How many beats did you hear? (a) One. (Students are given time to find the new sign on the rhythm sign display area.)
   c. When the sign is found, the note types are given. The rhythm syllable is given as ti tiri. The hand clap is shown. These are three uneven sounds on one beat.
   d. Teacher writes rhythm of Kookaburra on the board. Assigns a student to write the beats and tell why.

    e. Teacher writes the time signature as 2 with a heart under it. Assign a student to draw the bar lines.

    f. Class sings rhythm while teacher or student points to the beats.

(BEHAVIORAL OBJECTIVE 2)

6. WRITING ACTIVITY; method of procedure;

    a. Teacher writes A B A C A on the board. Each letter under the other with space between each. The time signature is 4 with a heart under it. Two measures for each section. Students tell teacher what to write in the measures for section A. Teacher reminds students that section B must be different from A. When A comes in again it must look like the first A section. Section C must be different from A and B. When composition is completed, class speaks the rhythm and claps the beat.

(BEHAVIORAL OBJECTIVE 4)

8. PLAY PARTY; "John Kanaka." (NEW)

9. CLOSURE; 1. Name the new song learned today. 2. Tell something about the new rhythm sign learned today.

10. GOOD-BYE; sung as;

Good-	bye	to	you.	(class echoes the same.)
s	m	m	d,	
ta	ti	ti	too-oo	

WRITE ON BOARD; 1. LEARN A NEW SONG. 2. LEARN A NEW RHYTHM SIGN. 3. WRITE AN ABACA RHYTHM COMPOSITION.

CHICKAMA, CHICKAMA

6
8
d d d d d d | d | 1, | s, |
Chick- a- ma, chick- a- ma | cra- | ney | crow.

d d d d | d | d | 1, | s, |
Went to the well to | wash | his | toe.

d d d d | d | d d 1, | s, |
When he got back his | chick- en was | gone.

What time old witch?
(SPOKEN)

"ONE."
(WITCH)

LESSON 29
INSTRUCTIONAL OBJECTIVES;
1. PRESENT D. C. al Fine.
2. PRACTICE identifying form.

BEHAVIORAL OBJECTIVES; students will;
1. Learn a new song. (INSTRUCTIONAL OBJECTIVE 1)
2. Learn a new music sign. (INSTRUCTIONAL OBJECTIVE 2)
3. Aurally and orally identify the form of several selections.
    (INSTRUCTIONAL OBJECTIVE 3)

MATERIALS; 1. SONG; "HUSH LITTLE BABY." 2. FLASH CARDS. 3. STATE ADOPTED
TEXT BOOK.

PROCEDURE;
1. GREETINGS; sung as; Hel-   lo   to   you.   (class echoes the same.)
                            s   m   m   d,
                            ta   ti   ti   too-oo

2. OPENING SONG; "Chicka Ma." On this they will;
    a. Sing the words and clap the beat.
    b. Do some form of part work.

3. FLASH CARD ACTIVITY; Select one or both.

____ a. Known rhythm cards.

____ b. Known solfege / rhythm cards.

STATE OBJECTIVES;

4. NEW SONG; "Hush Little Baby." On this they will;
    a. Learn the song by rote.
    b. Clap the beat while singing the words.
    c. Clap the way the words go.
    d. Use inner hearing to internalize the song.
(BEHAVIORAL OBJECTIVE 1)

5. PRESENT D.C. AL FINE; Define D. C. al Fine.
    a. Teacher selects several songs in the state adopted text that have a D. C. al Fine.
    b. Helps the children find the "Fine."
    c. Listen to the song and observes the D. C. al Fine.
    d. Tells the students that a D. C. al fine helps determine the form of a song.
    e. Has a short drill on identifying the form of a song with a D. C. al Fine.
(BEHAVIORAL OBJECTIVE 2 AND 3)

PAGE 2 LESSON 29

6. CHANGE OF PACE; Students will do the following play parties; "Bow, Wow, Wow", "John Kanaka" and "Sally Go Round The Sun."
(BEHAVIORAL OBJECTIVE 4)

7. CLOSURE; 1. Name the new song learned today. 2. Name the new music sign learned today.

8. GOOD-BYE; sung as; Good-   bye   to   you.   (class echoes the same.)
                              s   m   m   d,
                              ta   ti   ti   too-oo

WRITE ON BOARD; 1. LEARN A NEW SONG. 2. LEARN A NEW MUSIC SIGN.

HUSH LITTLE BABY

4	s,	m	m	m	f	m	r	r	r	
4	Hush	lit-	tle	ba-	by	don't	say	a	word.	

s,	s,	r	r	r	r	m	r	d	d
Pa-	pa's	gon-	na	buy	you	a	mock-	ing	bird.

s,	m	m	m	f	m	r	r	s,
It	can	whis-	tle	and	it	can	sing	and

s,	r	r	m	r	d	d
It	can	do	most	an-	y	thing.

1. Sing song all the way through. Then;
    LEAVE OUT   DO ACTIONS
2. Baby;   Rock arms.
3. Word;   Put finger over mouth.
4. Buy;   Slap pocket.
5. Bird;   Flutter finger in the air with a sweeping motion
6. Whistle;   Make whistle sound.
7. Sing;   Point to throat.
8. Most anything;   Hands make over under motion with palms down.

LESSON 29 GRADE_____ TEACHER_____

LESSON 30
INSTRUCTIONAL OBJECTIVES;
1. PREPARE tiri ti.
2. PRACTICE recognizing form.

BEHAVIORAL OBJECTIVES; students will;
1. Learn a new song. (INSTRUCTIONAL OBJECTIVE 1)
2. Take a test to show understanding of form. (INSTRUCTIONAL OBJECTIVE 2)

MATERIALS; 1. SONG; "RIDING IN THE BUGGY." 2. TEACHER SELECTED MATERIAL FOR FORM. 3. FLASH CARDS.

PROCEDURE;
1. GREETINGS; sung as; Hel-   lo   to   you.   (class echoes the same.)
                         s   m   m   d,
                         ta   ti   ti   too-oo

2. OPENING SONG; "Hush Little Baby." On this they will;
    a. Sing the words and clap the beat.
    b. Do some form of part work.

3. FLASH CARD ACTIVITY. Select one or both.

____ a. Known rhythm cards.

____ b. Known solfege /rhythm cards.

STATE OBJECTIVES;

4. NEW SONG; "Riding in the Buggy." On this they will;
    a. Learn the song by rote.
    b. Clap the beat while singing the words.
    c. Clap the way the words go.
    d. Use inner hearing to internalize the song.
(BEHAVIORAL OBJECTIVE 1)

5. TEST ON FORM; Teacher chooses method of presentation.
(BEHAVIORAL OBJECTIVE 2)

6. PLAY PARTY; "Button You Must Wander."

7. CLOSURE; 1. Name the new song learned today.

8. GOOD-BYE; sung as; Good-   bye   to   you.   (class echoes the same.)
                         s   m   m   d,
                         ta   ti   ti   too-oo

PAGE 2 LESSON 30

WRITE ON BOARD; 1. LEARN A NEW SONG. 2. REVIEW FORM.

RIDING IN A BUGGY

2/4	d	d	d	d	d	d	d	m		m	m	m		r	r	r	r	m		m	m
	Rid-ing	in	a	bug-gy	Miss			Mar-		y	Jane,	Miss		Mar-		y	Jane,	Miss	Mar-		y	Jane

d	d	d	d	d	d	d	m		m	m	m	m	m		r		m	d
Rid-ing	in	a	bug-gy	Miss			Mar-		y	Jane,	I'm	a	long		way		from	home.

d	d	m	s		d'	l	m	s
Who	calls	for	me?		Who	calls	for	me?

m	m	d	m	r	m	s	r	r	m	d
Who	calls	for	me	my	dar-	ling	who	calls	for	me?

FORMATION; Double circle. Hands joined in promenade position.

Partners walk the beat counterclockwise on the verse.
On the chorus, partners stop walking. Turn to face each other and do the following hand clapping pattern.
1. Pat own thighs.
2. Clap own hands together.
3. Clap hands with partner.
4. Clap own hands together.

LESSON 30 GRADE_____ TEACHER_____

LESSON 31
INSTRUCTIONAL OBJECTIVES;
1. PREPARE low la.
2. PRACTICE deriving rhythm, melody and form of a familiar song.

BEHAVIORAL OBJECTIVES; students will;
1. Learn a new song. (INSTRUCTIONAL OBJECTIVE 1)
2. Derive the rhythm, melody, and form of a familiar song.
   (INSTRUCTIONAL OBJECTIVE 2)

MATERIALS; 1. SONG; "CUMBERLAND GAP." 2. PENCILS AND PAPER. 3. FLASH CARDS.

PROCEDURE;
1. GREETINGS; sung as; Hel-　lo　　to　　you.　　　　　　(class echoes the same.)
　　　　　　　　　　　　　　s　　m　　r　　d,
　　　　　　　　　　　　　　ta　　ti　　ti　　too-oo

2. OPENING SONG; "Riding in the Buggy." On this they will;
   a. Sing the words and clap the beat.
   b. Do some form of partwork.

3. FLASH CARD ACTIVITY; Select one or both.

___ a. Known rhythm cards.

___ b. Known solfege / rhythm cards.

STATE OBJECTIVES;

4. NEW SONG; "Cumberland Gap." On this they will;
   a. Learn the song by rote.
   b. Clap beat and sing the words.
   c. Clap and sing the rhythm syllables.
   d. Use inner hearing to internalize the song.
(BEHAVIORAL OBJECTIVE 1)

5. PRACTICE DERIVING RHYTHM AND FORM; Presentation song "Who's That."
   a. Class sings song.
   b. Class derives rhythm. Teacher writes this on the board four lines, two measures
      each with two beats in each measure. Time signature written as a 2 with a heart
      under it.
   c. Class derives form.
   d. Class identifies the rhythm signs and writes the heart beats.
(BEHAVIORAL OBJECTIVE 2)

6. WRITING ACTIVITY;
    a. Class copies material from the board for study purposes.
    b. Homework assignment; Be able to sing and clap the rhythm syllables. Then sing the pitch syllables and do the hand signs next class session.

7. PLAY PARTIES; "Bow, Wow, Wow," "John Kanaka", and "Button You Must Wander."

8. CLOSURE; 1. Name the new song learned today. 2. Students are reminded of home work.

9. GOOD-BYE; sung as; Good-   bye   to   you   (class echoes the same.)
                          s   m   r   d,
                          ta   ti   ti   too-oo

WRITE ON BOARD; 1. LEARN A NEW SONG. 2. REVIEW DERIVING RHYTHM AND FORM.
3. PRACTICE SEVERAL PLAY PARTIES.

CUMBERLAND GAP

2. Cumberland Gap's a mighty fine place.
    Can't get water for to wash your face.

3. Cumberland Gap with it's cliffs and rocks.
    Home of the panther, bear and fox.

LESSON 31 GRADE_____ TEACHER_____

LESSON 32
INSTRUCTIONAL OBJECTIVES;
1. PREPARE low la and low so.
2. PRESENT tiri ti.
3. PRACTICE (a) Singing and clapping rhythm syllables. (b) Singing pitch syllables and making the hand signs.

BEHAVIORAL OBJECTIVES; students will;
1. Learn a new song. (INSTRUCTIONAL OBJECTIVE 1)
2. Learn a new rhythm sign and its syllable. (INSTRUCTIONAL OBJECTIVE 2)
3. Sing and clap the rhythm syllables of a familiar song. Then sing the pitch syllables and do the hand sings for the same song. (INSTRUCTIONAL OBJECTIVE 3)

MATERIALS; 1. SONG; "I'VE BEEN TO HARLEM." 2. TWO SIXTEENTHS AND ONE EIGHTH NOTE COMBINATION ON THE RHYTHM DISPLAY AREA. 3. FLASH CARDS.

PROCEDURE;
1. GREETINGS; sung as; Hel-   lo   to   you.   (class echoes the same.)
                        s   m   r   d,
                        ta   ti   ti   too-oo

2. OPENING SONG; "Cumberland Gap." On this they will;
   a. Sing the words and clap the beat.
   b. Do some form of part work.

3. FLASH CARD ACTIVITY; Select one or both.

___ a. Known rhythm cards.

___ b. Known solfege / rhythm cards.

STATE OBJECTIVES;

4. NEW SONG; "I've Been To Harlem." On this they will;
   a. Learn the song by rote.
   b. Clap beat and sing the words.
   c. Clap and sing the rhythm syllables.
   d. Use inner hearing to internalize the song.
(BEHAVIORAL OBJECTIVE 1)

5. PRESENT TIRI TI; Presentation song "Riding in a Buggy."
   a. Class sings song.
   b. Teacher targets "buggy miss."
       (q) How many sounds did you hear? (a) 3.
       (q) How many beats did you hear? (a) 1.
   c. Class is given time to find the tiri ti sign (Three uneven sounds for one beat.)
   d. When the sign is found the note types are given. The rhythm syllable is given. The clap is shown.

    e. Teacher places rhythm of the first line of "Riding in the Buggy" on the board. Students tell teacher where to place heart beats and why they are placed there. Then the class claps and sings the rhythm syllables.

(BEHAVIORAL OBJECTIVE 2)

6. STUDENT PERFORMANCE. Presentation song "Who's That."
    a. Class sings song.
    b. Sings and claps rhythm syllables.
    c. Class sings the pitch syllables and makes the hand signs.
    d. Each student does the same individually and is given a grade.

(BEHAVIORAL OBJECTIVE 3)

7. CLOSURE; 1. Name the new song learned today. 2. Tell something about the new rhythm sign learned today.

8. GOOD-BYE; sung as; Good- bye to you.   (class echoes the same.)
                              s   m   r   d,
                            ta   ti ti too-oo

WRITE ON BOARD; 1. LEARN A NEW SONG. 2. LEARN A NEW RHYTHM SIGN.
3. PERFORM THE RHYTHM AND PITCH FOR "WHO'S THAT."

I'VE BEEN TO HARLEM

d	d	d	l,	s,	d	d	d	l,	s,	d	d	d	m	s		
I've	been	to	Har-	lem.	I've	been	to	Do-	ver.	I've	travel-	ed	this	wide		

m	d	s	m	s	m	s	m	d	d	l,	s,
world	all	o-	ver,	o-	ver,	o-	ver	three	times	o-	ver.

d	d	d	m	m	s	s	m	m	r	r	d	d	m	s	s
Drink	all	the	bran-	dy	wine	and	turn	the	glas-	ses	o-	ver.	Sail-	ing	east.

m	s	s		l	s	l	s	m	m	r
Sail-	ing	west.		Sail-	ing	o-	ver	the	o-	cean.

d	d	d	l,	s,	l,	d	d	d	d	l,	s,	l,	d	m	s	m	d
Bet-	ter	watch	out	when	the	boat	be-	gins	to	rock	or	you'll	lose	your	girl	in	the

r	d
o-	cean.

TERMINAL 8 AFTER LESSON 32

BEHAVIORAL OBJECTIVES; students will;
1. Define music terms.
2. Identify rhythm signs.
3. Name music symbols.

MATERIALS; 1. PENCILS AND TERMINAL EIGHT WORKSHEETS. 2. BINDERS.

PROCEDURE;
1. GREETINGS; sung as; Hel-   lo   to   you.   (class echoes the same.)
                       s   m   r   d,
                       ta   ti   ti   too-oo

2. OPENING SONG; "I've Been To Harlem." On this they will;
   a. Sing the words, sing the rhythm and clap beat with each.
   b. Do some form of part work.

SPONGE ACTIVITY;

STATE OBJECTIVES;

3. WORKSHEET ACTIVITY; Pass out pencils and Terminal 8 worksheet. Students discuss
   written instructions and then fill out the worksheet independently.
(BEHAVIORAL OBJECTIVES 1, 2, AND 3).

4. STUDENT PERFORMANCE; Class sings all do re me so la songs in the binder using
rhythm syllables, pitch syllables and pitch syllables with hand signs.

5. PLAY PARTY; "Riding In A Buggy". (NEW)

6. GOOD-BYE; sung as; Good-   bye   to   you.   (class echoes the same.)
                      s   m   r   d,
                      ta   ti   ti   too-oo

WRITE ON BOARD; 1. FILL IN TERMINAL EIGHT WORKSHEET.

TERMINAL 8   GRADE _____ TEACHER_____

NAME _____ CLASS _____ DATE _____

Match the words or symbols with a letter in front of a sentence that tells what it is.

_____ 1. Slur

a. The format of a music selection.

_____ 2. Tone Color

b. Half note. One sound for two beats.

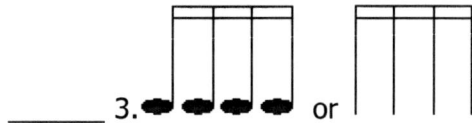
_____ 3.   or

c. A curved line over two or more different notes sung on one word.

_____ 4. Form

d. Go back to the beginning and stop at fine.

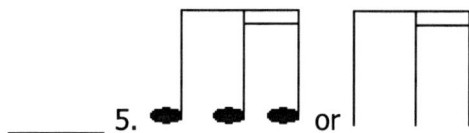
_____ 5.   or

e. The distinguished sound of instruments or voices.

_____ 6. D. C. al Fine

f. One eighth note and two sixteenths or ti tiri. Three uneven sounds for one beat.

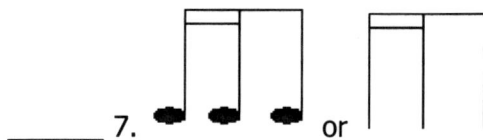
_____ 7.   or

g. A curved line connecting two or more notes on the same pitch making the sound longer.

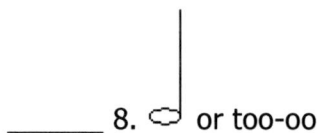
_____ 8.   or too-oo

h. Two sixteenths and one eighth note or tiri ti. Three uneven sounds on one beat.

_____ 9. Tie

i. Four sixteenth notes of tiritiri. Four sounds for one beat.

_____ 10. ▄▄

j. Half rest. No sound for two beats.

TERMINAL 8 WORKSHEET NO. ONE OF ONE.

LESSON 33
INSTRUCTIONAL OBJECTIVES;
1. PREPARE high do.
2. PRESENT low la on the tone ladder.
3. PRESENT stepping, skipping and repeat on the staff.

BEHAVIORAL OBJECTIVES; students will;
1. Learn a new song. (INSTRUCTIONAL OBJECTIVE 1)
2. Learn a new pitch syllable. (INSTRUCTIONAL OBJECTIVE 2)
3. Visually identify stepping, skipping and repeated tones on the staff.
   (INSTRUCTIONAL OBJECTIVE 3)

MATERIALS; 1. SONG; "CAMPTOWN LADIES." 2. MAGNETIC STAFF BOARD AND
PROPERTIES. 3. FLASH CARDS.

PROCEDURE;
1. GREETINGS; sung as; Hel-   lo   to   you.   (class echoes the same.)
                          s   m   r   d,
                          ta   ti   ti   too-oo

2. OPENING SONG; "I've Been To Harlem." On this they will;
   a. Sing the words and clap the beat.
   b. Do some form of part work.

3. FLASH CARD ACTIVITY. Select one or both.

___ a. Known rhythm cards.

___ b. Known solfege / rhythm cards.

STATE OBJECTIVES;

4. NEW SONG; "Camptown Ladies." On this they will;
   a. Learn the song by rote.
   b. Sing the words and clap the beat.
   c. Clap the way the words go.
   d. Use inner hearing to internalize the song.
(BEHAVIORAL OBJECTIVE 1)

5. PRESENT LOW LA ON THE TONE LADDER.
   Presentation song "Cumberland Gap."
   a. Class sings song.
   b. Derives rhythm.
   c. Uses the tone ladder and a question mark to derive the melody.
   d. (q) Is the new tone higher or lower than do? (a) Lower.
   e. (q) Is the new tone a step or a skip down from do? (Teacher sings example of a
      step down and a skip down from do.) (a) a skip down.

    f. Students discuss moving down on the tone ladder and find the new tone is low la. The hand sign is shown. 1, is placed on the tone ladder. Class sings song again. First singing the pitch syllables then singing the pitch syllables and making the hand signs.

(BEHAVIORAL OBJECTIVE 2)

6. PRESENT STEPPING, SKIPPING AND REPEAT ON THE STAFF.
    Presentation song" "Great Big House".
    a. Class sings song with words and then with pitch syllables.
    b. Teacher places pitches on the staff.
    c. Students are given examples of step, skip and repeat.
    d. Students visually identify tones as moving by steps, skips or repeats.

(BEHAVIORAL OBJECTIVE 3)

7. CLOSURE; 1. Name the new song learned today. 2. Name the new pitch syllable learned today. 3. Tell how notes move on the staff.

8. GOOD-BYE; sung as; Good- bye to you.   (class echoes the same.)
                    d,   1,   1,   d,
                    ta   ti   ti   too-oo

WRITE ON BOARD; 1. LEARN A NEW SONG. 2. LEARN A NEW PITCH SYLLABLE.
3. LEARN ABOUT STEP, SKIP, AND REPEAT ON THE STAFF.

CAMPTOWN LADIES

s	s	m	s	l	s	m	m	r.	m	r.
Camp-	town	la-	dies	sing	this	song	doo	dah	doo	dah.

s	s	m	s	l	s	m	r	m	r	d
Camp-	town	race-	track	five	miles	long	oh	doo	dah	day.

d.	d	m	s	d'	l.	l	d'	l	s
Go-	na	run	all	night.	Go-	na	run	all	day.

s	s	m	m	s	s	l	s	m	r	m	f	m	r	r	d
Bet	my	money	on	the	bob	tail	nag	some-bo-	dy	bet	on	the	bay.

LESSON 34
INSTRUCTIONAL OBJECTIVES;
1. PREPARE low so.
2. PRESENT D. S. al Fine.
3. PRACTICE (a) Singing while clapping an ostinato. (b) Singing while playing an ostinato.

BEHAVIORAL OBJECTIVES; students will;
1. Learn a new song. (INSTRUCTIONAL OBJECTIVE 1)
2. Learn about D. S. al Fine. (INSTRUCTIONAL OBJECTIVE 2)
3. Clap a rhythm ostinato while singing a familiar song.
   (INSTRUCTIONAL OBJECTIVE 3a)
   Play a skipping pattern as an ostinato while singing a familiar song.
   (INSTRUCTIONAL OBJECTIVE 3b)

MATERIALS; 1. SONG; "SCOTLAND'S BURNING." 2. BIG XYLOPHONE AND TWO MELODY BELLS D AND D'. 3. FLASH CARDS.

PROCEDURE;
1. GREETING; sung as;

Hel-	lo	to	you	(class echoes the same.)
d,	1,	1,	d,	
ta	ti	ti	too-oo	

2. OPENING SONG; "Camptown Races". On this they will;
   a. Sing the words and clap the beat.
   b. Do some form or part work.

3. FLASH CARD ACTIVITY; Select one or both.
___ a. Known rhythm cards.

___ b. Known solfege / rhythm cards.

STATE OBJECTIVES;

4. NEW SONG; "Scotland's Burning." On this they will;
   a. Learn the song by rote.
   b. Clap the beat while singing the words.
   c. Sing and clap the rhythm syllables.
   d. Use inner hearing to internalize the song.
(BEHAVIORAL OBJECTIVE 1)

5. PRESENT D. S. al Fine; Presentation song "Button You Must Wander."
   a. Class sings song.
   b. Derives rhythm through singing.
   c. Teacher writes rhythm on the board with time signature written as a four with a heart under it. All together class speaks about beats and rhythm. Example; one sound for one beat. Teacher writes beats. All together class counts beats and teacher writes in bar lines. Example; 1, 2, 3, 4, bar line.

111

PAGE 2 LESSON 34

   d. Derives the form.
   e. Teacher explains D. S. al Fine by pointing out that line two and four are the same. Places a D. S. al Fine at the end of line three. Erases line four and puts the D. S. al Fine sign at the beginning of line two. Places a double bar line and the word FINE at the end of line two. Explains that D. S. al Fine means to go back to the sign and stop at the Fine. The form does not change.
   f. Students sing song again observing the D. S. al Fine.
(BEHAVIORAL OBJECTIVE 2)

6. PRESENT OSTINATO; Teacher defines ostinato. Teacher gives example of a rhythm ostinato. Class sings "Great Big House" while clapping a rhythm ostinato.
(BEHAVIORAL OBJECTIVE 3a)
Teacher gives an example of a melodic ostinato. Students are given an opportunity to sing "Great Big House" and play the melodic ostinato.
(BEHAVIORAL OBJECTIVE 3b)

7. CLOSURE; 1. Name the new song learned today. 2. Define D. S. al fine. 3. Define Ostinato. 4. Assign homework; definitions for harmony, round, and unison. 5. Be able to sing "Great Big House" and play or clap an ostinato.

8. GOOD-BYE; sung as; Good- bye to you. (class echoes the same.)
                    d, 1, 1, d,
                    ta ti ti too-oo

WRITE ON BOARD; 1. LEARN A NEW SONG. 2. LEARN A NEW MUSIC SIGN. 3. PLAY AN OSTINATO WHILE SINGING A FAMILIAR SONG.

SCOTLAND'S BURNING

2	s,	s,	d	d		s,	s,	d	d
4	Scot-	land's burn-	ing		Scot-	land's burn-	ing.

r	m	r	m
Look	out!	Look	out!

s	s	s	s
Fire!	Fire!	Fire!	Fire!

s,	s,	d	d	s,	s,	d	d
Pour	on	wa-	ter.	Pour	on	wa-	ter.

LESSON 35
INSTRUCTIONAL OBJECTIVES;
1. PREPARE tum ti.
2. PRESENT measure counts.
3. PRACTICE harmony elements.

BEHAVIORAL OBJECTIVES; students will;
1. Learn a new song. (INSTRUCTIONAL OBJECTIVE 1)
2. Replace heart beats with measure counts. (INSTRUCTIONAL OBJECTIVE 2)
3. Demonstrate ability to sing a song. (INSTRUCTIONAL OBJECTIVE 3)
   a. In unison.
   b. As a two part round.
   c. With an ostinato.

MATERIALS; 1. SONG; "CHAIRS TO MEND." 2. BIG XYLOPHONE. 3. TWO MELODY
BELLS, D AND D'. 4. FLASH CARDS.

PROCEDURE;
1. GREETING; sung as; Hel-   lo   to   you.   (class echoes the same.)
                        s   m   m   d,
                        ta   ti   ti   too-oo

2. OPENING SONG; "Scotland's Burning". On this they will;
   a. Sing the words and clap the beat.
   b. Sing as a round.

3. FLASH CARD ACTIVITY; Select one or both.

___ a. Known rhythm cards.

___ b. Known solfege / rhythm cards.

STATE OBJECTIVES;

4. NEW SONG; "Chairs to Mend." On this they will;
   a. Learn the song by rote.
   b. Clap the beat and sing the words.
   c. Clap the way the words go.
   d. Use inner hearing to internalize the song.
(BEHAVIORAL OBJECTIVE 1)

5. RHYTHM STUDY; Presentation song "Button You Must Wander."
   a. Class sings song, derives rhythm, places heartbeats and bar lines.
   b. Teacher demonstrates how to replace heartbeats with measure counts filling in the
      first measure only.
   c. Students show understanding of this by completing the writing of measure counts
      for the whole song.
(BEHAVIORAL OBJECTIVE 2)

PAGE 2 LESSON 35

6. HARMONY STUDY; Presentation song "Great Big House."
   a. Class gives definitions of the following terms; harmony, unison, round, and ostinato.
   b. Class is lead to apply these terms by singing; in unison; a round; singing while clapping an ostinato; singing a song while playing an ostinato on the bells.
(BEHAVIORAL OBJECTIVE 3)

7. CLOSURE; 1. Give name of new song learned today. 2. Class tells what the top number of a time signature means. 3. Class sings "Great Big House" with ostinatos.

8. GOOD-BYE; sung as; Good-   bye   to   you.   (class echoes the same.)
                       s   m   m   d,
                     ta   ti   ti   too-oo

WRITE ON BOARD; 1. LEARN A NEW SONG. 2. LEARN ABOUT MEASURE COUNTS. 3. LEARN THREE ELEMENTS OF HARMONY.

CHAIRS TO MEND

4	s	f	m	1	s	f	m
4	Chairs	to	mend	old	Chairs	to	mend.

m	r	d	f	m	r	d
Mack-	er-	el	fresh	Mack-	er-	el.

d	d	s,	s,	d	d
Old	Rags	an-	y	Old	Rags.

TERMINAL 9 AFTER LESSON 35

BEHAVIORAL OBJECTIVES; students will;
1. Write measure counts, bar lines and double bar lines for a rhythm exercise.
2. Write the definition for D. S. al Fine.
3. Demonstrate an understanding of D. S. al Fine.

MATERIALS; 1. TERMINAL 9 WORKSHEETS AND PENCILS.

PROCEDURE;
1. GREETING; sung as; Hel- lo to you.   (class echoes the same.)
                        s   m   m   d,
                        ta   ti   ti   too-oo

2. OPENING SONG; "Chairs to Mend." On this they will;
    a. Sing the words, sing the rhythm and clap the rhythm on each.
    b. Do some form of part work.

SPONGE ACTIVITY;

STATE OBJECTIVES;

3. WORKSHEET ACTIVITY. Class is lead into a brief review of how to write measure counts. Pencils and terminal 9 worksheets are passed out. Class reads the directions together and then work independently to fill out worksheets.
(BEHAVIORAL OBJECTIVE 1 AND 2)

4. STUDENT PERFORMANCE OF D. S AL FINE; Presentation song "Button You Must Wander."
    a. Class sings song.
    b. Derives rhythm.
    c. Rhythm is written on the board with the D. S. al Fine at the end of the third line. The sign at the beginning of the second line and FINE at the end of the second line with a double bar line and the word FINE.
    d. Each student will sing the rhythm, observe the D. S. al Fine and is given a grade.
(BEHAVIORAL OBJECTIVE 3)

5. GOOD-BYE; sung as; Good- bye to you.   (class echoes the same.)
                        s   m   m   d,
                        ta   ti   ti   too-oo

WRITE ON BOARD; 1. FILL IN A WORKSHEET. 2. DEMONSTRATE AN UNDERSTANDING OF D. S. AL FINE.

TERMINAL 9   GRADE _____ TEACHER_____

NAME _____ CLASS _____ DATE _____

1. Circle the top number of the time signature.
2. Write the measure counts.
3. Place bar lines according to the top number of the time signature. Be sure to place the double bar line.

1.

2.

3.

DEFINE D. S. al Fine._____

_____

LESSON 36
INSTRUCTIONAL OBJECTIVES;
1. PREPARE the dotted half note and three four time.
2. PRESENT low la on the staff.
3. PRACTICE reading pitch syllables on the staff.

BEHAVIORAL OBJECTIVES; students will;
1. Learn a new song. (INSTRUCTIONAL OBJECTIVE 1)
2. Form a generalization statement for low la. (INSTRUCTIONAL OBJECTIVE 2)
3. Sing pitch syllables of a familiar song on the staff. (INSTRUCTIONAL OBJECTIVE 3)

MATERIALS; 1. SONG; "LOVELY EVENING." 2. MAGNETIC STAFF AND PROPERTIES.
3. FLASH CARDS.

PROCEDURE;
1. GREETING; sung as; Hel- lo   to   you.   (class echoes the same.)
                         d,   s,   s,   d,
                         ta   ti   ti   too-oo

2. OPENING SONG; "Chairs To Mend". On this they will;
    a. Sing the words and clap the beat.
    b. Sing as a round.

3. FLASH CARD ACTIVITY; Select one or both.

___ a. Known rhythm cards.

___ b. Known solfege /rhythm cards.

STATE OBJECTIVES

4. NEW SONG; "Lovely Evening". On this they will;
    a. Learn the song by rote.
    b. Teacher gives new way to clap the beat and sing the words. (Tap desk one time
        then clap hands two times.) Students do the new beat clap while singing the
        words.
    c. Use inner hearing to internalize the song.
(BEHAVIORAL OBJECTIVE 1)

5. PRESENT LOW LA ON THE STAFF. Presentation song "Cumeberland Gap".
    a. Class sings song.
    b. Derives rhythm by singing the rhythm syllables. This is written on the board.
    c. Derives the melody by singing the pitch syllables.
    d. Teacher puts the do clef in the first space and writes the notes for "Cumberland
        Gap" on the magnetic staff.
    e. Leads a discussion about staff relationship of low la to do.
(BEHAVIORAL OBJECTIVE 2)

6. MUSIC PERFORMANCE; Students will sing pitch syllables to "Cumberland Gap" while pointing to notes on the magnetic staff. (INDIVIDUALLY)
(BEHAVIORAL OBJECTIVE 3)

7. CLOSURE; 1. Name of the new song learned today. 2. Generalization statement for low la. 3. Assign homework; Practice singing "Cumberland GAP" six ways.
        a. Words. b. Rhythm. c. Pitch syllables. d. Pitch syllables with hand signs. e. On the tone ladder. f. On the staff.

8. GOOD-BYE; sung as; Good-   bye   to   you.   (class echoes the same.)
                         d,   1,   1,   d,
                         ta   ti   ti   too-oo

WRITE ON BOARD; 1. LEARN A NEW SONG. 2. PLACE LOW LA ON THE STAFF. 3. SING "CUMBERLAND GAP" ON THE STAFF.

LOVELY EVENING

3
4

d	r	m	d	f	m	m — r	d
Oh	how	love-	ly	is	the	eve -	ning,

f	m	m — r	d	m	f	s	m
is	the	eve -	ning.	When	the	bells	are

l	s	s — f	m	l	s	s — f	m
sweet-	ly	ring -	ing.	sweet-	ly	ring -	ing.

d	d	d	d
Ding	Dong	Ding	Dong

d	d
Ding	Dong.

TERMINAL 10 AFTER LESSON 36

BEHAVIORAL OBJECTIVES; students will;
1. Sing a familiar song six ways.
   a. Words.
   b. Rhythm syllables.
   c. Pitch syllables.
   d. Pitch syllables and hand sings.
   e. On the tone ladder.
   f. On the staff.

MATERIALS; 1. 1, d r m s 1 TONE LADDER DRAWN ON BOARD. 2. NOTES OF SONG ON THE MAGNETIC STAFF.

PROCEDURE;
1. GREETING; sung as; Hel- lo   to   you.   (class echoes the same.)
                        d,   s,   s,   d,
                        ta   ti   ti   too-oo

2. OPENING SONG; "Lovely Evening". On this they will;
   a. Sing the words and clap the beat.
   b. Do some form of part work.

SPONGE ACTIVITY;

STATE OBJECTIVES;

3. STUDENT PERFORMANCE; Presentation song "Cumberland Gap."
   a. Class sings the song six ways.
   b. Each student is given an opportunity to sing the song six ways and is given a grade.
(BEHAVIORAL OBJECTIVE 1)

4. GOOD-BYE; sung as; Good- bye to   you.   (class echoes the same.)
                        d,   s,   s,   d,
                        ta   ti   ti   too-oo

WRITE ON BOARD; 1. SING "CUMBERLAND GAP" SIX WAYS.

TERMINAL 10   GRADE _____ TEACHER_____

LESSON 37

INSTRUCTIONAL OBJECTIVES;
1. PREPARE the dotted half note.
2. PRESENT low so on the tone ladder.

BEHAVIORAL OBJECTIVES; students will;
1. Learn a new song. (INSTRUCTIONAL OBJECTIVE 1)
2. Learn a new pitch syllable. (INSTRUCTIONAL OBJECTIVE 2)

MATERIALS; 1. SONG; "THREE ROGUES." (Teacher may want to have copies for class)
2. MAGNETIC S,. 3. FLASH CARDS. 4. BINDERS.

PROCEDURE;
1. GREETING; sung as; Hel- lo   to   you.   (class echoes the same.)
                            d,   1,   1,   d,
                            ta   ti   ti   too-oo

2. OPENING SONG; "Lovely Evening." On this they will;
    a. Sing the words and clap the beat.
    b. Sing as a round or a canon.

3. FLASH CARD ACTIVITY; Select one or both.

___ a. Known rhythm cards.

___ b. Known solfege / rhythm cards.

STATE OBJECTIVES;

4. NEW SONG; "Three Rogues." On this they will;
    a. Learn what a ballad is.
    b. Learn the song by rote.
    c. Clap the beat while singing the words.
    d. Clap the way the words go.
    e. Use inner hearing to internalize the song.
(BEHAVIORAL OBJECTIVE 1)

5. PRESENT LOW SO ON THE TONE LADDER;
    Presentation song "I've Been To Harlem."
    a. Class sings song.
    b. Derives rhythm for first two measures.
    c. Uses tone ladder and question mark to derive melody and find the new tone.
    d. Identifies the new pitch syllable as low so. The hand sign is shown. Low so is
        placed on the tone ladder.
    e. Class sings first two measures with pitch syllables while teacher points to steps on
        the tone ladder.

    f.   Finds the following songs in binder; 1. "Chicka Ma". 2. "Scotland's Burning". 3. "John Kanaka". 4. "Weavily Wheat". Sings the words and then the pitch syllables.

(BEHAVIORAL OBJECTIVE 2)

6.   PLAY PARTIES; 1. WEAVILY WHEAT 2. JOHN KANAKA.

7.   CLOSURE; 1. Name the new song learned today. Give the definition of a Ballad. 3. Name the new pitch syllable.

8.   GOOD-BYE; sung as; Good-   bye   to   you.   (class echoes the same.)

                           d,   s,   s,   d,

                           ta   ti   ti   too-oo

WRITE ON BOARD; 1. LEARN A NEW SONG. 2. LEARN A NEW PITCH SYLLABLE. 3. PERFORM THREE PLAY PARTIES.

PAGE 3 LESSON 37

THE THREE ROGUES

2.   The first he was a miller. The second he was a weaver. And the third he was a little tailor boy with the broadcloth under his arm. With the broadcloth under his arm. With the broadcloth under his arm. And the third he was a little tailor boy with the broadcloth under his arm.

3.   The miller he stole corn. The weaver he stole yarn. And the little tailor boy stole broadcloth enough to keep the three rogues warm. To keep the three rogues warm. To keep the three rogues warm. And the little tailor boy stole broadcloth enough to keep the three rogues warm.

4.   The miller got drowned in his dam. The weaver got hung in his yarn. And the devil caught the little tailor boy with the broadcloth under his arm. With the broadcloth under his arm. With the broadcloth under his arm. And the devil caught the little tailor boy with the broadcloth under his arm.

LESSON 38
INSTRUCTIONAL OBJECTIVES;
1. PREPARE la pentatonic.
2. PRESENT the dotted half note.

BEHAVIORAL OBJECTIVES; students will;
1. Learn a new song. (INSTRUCTIONAL OBJECTIVE 1)
2. Learn a new rhythm sign and its syllable. (INSTRUCTIONAL OBJECTIVE 2)

MATERIALS; 1. SONG; "MY GOOD OLD MAN." (Teacher may want to have copies for class) 2. MAGNETIC BOARD AND PROPERTIES. 3. FLASH CARDS.

PROCEDURE;
1. GREETING; sung as; Hel- lo   to   you.   (class echoes the same.)
                       d,   1,   s,   d,
                       ta   ti   ti   too-oo

2. OPENING SONG; "The Three Rogues." On this they will;
   a. Sing the words and clap the beat.
   b. Do some form of part work.

3. FLASH CARD ACTIVITY; Select one or both.

___ a. Known rhythm cards.

___ b. Known solfege / rhythm cards.

STATE OBJECTIVES;

4. NEW SONG; "My Good Old Man." On this they will;
   a. Learn the song by rote.
   b. Clap the beat while singing the words.
   c. Clap the way the words go.
   d. Use inner hearing to internalize the song.
(BEHAVIORAL OBJECTIVE 1)

5. PRESENT THE DOTTED HALF NOTE; Presentation song "Lovely Evening."
   a. Class sings song.
   b. Teacher targets the word "Ding."
   c. Students are instructed to identify the number of sounds and beats heard.
   d. After some discussion the name dotted half note is given and the hand clap is shown as clap slide slide. The rhythm syllable is given as too-oo-e.
   e. The rhythm for "Lovely Evening" is written on the board. The class sings and claps the rhythm syllables.
(BEHAVIORAL OBJECTIVE 2)

6. PLAY PARTIES; Review all that have been learned.

7. CLOSURE; 1. Name the new song learned today. 2. Tell something about the new rhythm sign learned today.
8. GOOD-BYE; sung as; Good-   bye   to   you.   (class echoes the same.)
                               d,   1,   s,   d,
                               ta   ti   ti   too-oo

WRITE ON BOARD; 1. LEARN A NEW SONG. 2. LEARN A NEW RHYTHM SIGN.

MY GOOD OLD MAN

2/4 1, Where	1, are	d you	m go-	m ing	d my	m good	d old	1, man?
m Where	m are	s you	1 go-	1 ing	m my	s su-	s gar	r my m lamb?
1, Best	m old	r man	d in	d the	1, world.			

1. (spoken; to market.)
2. What will you buy there, my good old man?
   What will you buy there my sugar my lamb?
   Best old man in the world.
   (spoken; Bushel of eggs.)

3. Bushel will kill you, my good old man.
   Bushel will kill you, my sugar my lamb.
   Best old man in the world.
   (spoken; Don't care if it does.)

4. What for to die, my good old man.
   What for to die, my sugar my lamb.
   Best old man in the world.
   (spoken; So I can haunt you.)

5. Why will you haunt me, my good old man.
   Why will you haunt me, my sugar my lamb.
   Best old man in the world.
   (spoken: So I can always be near you.)

LESSON 38 GRADE_____ TEACHER_____

LESSON 39
INSTRUCTIONAL OBJECTIVES;
1. PREPARE high do.
2. PRESENT (a) Syn co pa. (b) Place low so on the staff.
3. PRACTICE making a G clef.

BEHAVIORAL OBJECTIVES; students will;
1. Learn a new song. (INSTRUCTIONAL OBJECTIVE 1)
2. Learn a new rhythm sign and it's syllable. (INSTRUCTIONAL OBJECTIVE 2)
3. Derive a generalization statement for low so. (INSTRUCTIONAL OBJECTIVE 3)
4. Learn to make a G clef. (INSTRUCTIONAL OBJECTIVE 4)

MATERIALS; 1. SONG; "TIDEO". 2. MAGNETIC STAFF WITH LEGER LINES. 3. CHALK BOARDS, ERASERS AND CHALK. 4. FLASH CARDS.

PROCEDURE;
1. GREETING; sung as; Hel-   lo   to   you   (class echoes the same.)
                         d,   s,   s,   d,
                         ta   ti   ti   too-oo

2. OPENING SONG; "My Good Old Man". On this they will;
   a. Sing the words and clap the beat.
   b. Do some form of part work.

3. FLASH CARD ACTIVITY; Select one or both.

___ a. Known rhythm cards.

___ b. Known solfege / rhythm cards.

STATE OBJECTIVES;

4. NEW SONG; "Tideo". On this the students will;
   a. Learn the song by rote.
   b. Clap the beat while singing the words.
   c. Clap and sing the rhythm syllables.
   d. Use inner hearing to internalize the song.
(BEHAVIORAL OBJECTIVE 1)

5. PRESENT SYN CO PA; Presentation song "Weavily Wheat".
   a. Class sings song.
   b. Teacher sings the words and claps the beats of the phrase, "don't want your".
   c. Class is given time to identify the new rhythm sign by the number of sounds and beats heard.
   d. After the sign is found the rhythm syllable syn co pa is given. The note types are given. The hand clap is shown.
   e. Teacher writes syn co pa rhythm on board and shows class how to write the beats.

    f. Class finds "Weavily Wheat," "Alabama Gal," and "My Good Old Man" in the binder. Sings and claps the rhythm syllables. Then claps the beat and sings the rhythm syllables.

(BEHAVIORAL OBJECTIVE 2)

6. PRESENT LOW SO ON THE STAFF;
Presentation song "Scotland's Burning".
    a. Class sings song using words, rhythm syllables and then pitch syllables. (Rhythm signs and pitch letters are written on the board.
    b. Teacher then gives instructions for writing this song on the staff. The do clef is placed in first space. Students discuss tones that move down the staff below do. Discovers the fact that a line has to be added for low so. Students are reminded that this is a leger line.
    c. Teacher writes notes on the magnetic staff assisted by the class.
    d. Class sings the pitch syllables while the teacher or a student points to the notes on the staff.

(BEHAVIORAL OBJECTIVE 3)

7. WRITING ACTIVITY; Students will be given instruction for making a G clef.
(BEHAVIORAL OBJECTIVE 4)

8. CLOSURE; 1. Name the new song learned today. 2. Tell something about the new rhythm sign learned today. 3. State the generalization statement for low so. 4. What is a leger line?

9. GOOD-BYE; sung as;

Good-	bye	to	you.	(class echoes the same.)
d,	s,	s,	d,	
ta	ti	ti	too-oo	

WRITE ON BOARD; 1. LEARN A NEW SONG. 2. LEARN A NEW RHYTHM SIGN. 3. PLACE LOW SO ON THE STAFF. 5. LEARN TO MAKE A G CLEF.

TIDEO

2
4

m	s	s	l	m	s	s		m	s	s	l	m	r	d,
Pass	one	win-	dow	ti-	de-	o.		Pass	two	win-	dows	ti	de-	o.

m	s	s	l	m	s	s		m	s	s	s	s	l	m	r	d,
Pass	three	win-	dows	ti-	de-	o		Jin-gle	at	the	win-	dow	ti-	de	o.

m	s	d'		m	s	d'		m	s	s	s	s	l	m	r	d,
Ti-	de-	o.		Ti-	de-	o.		Jin-gle	at	the	win-	dow	ti-	de-	o.

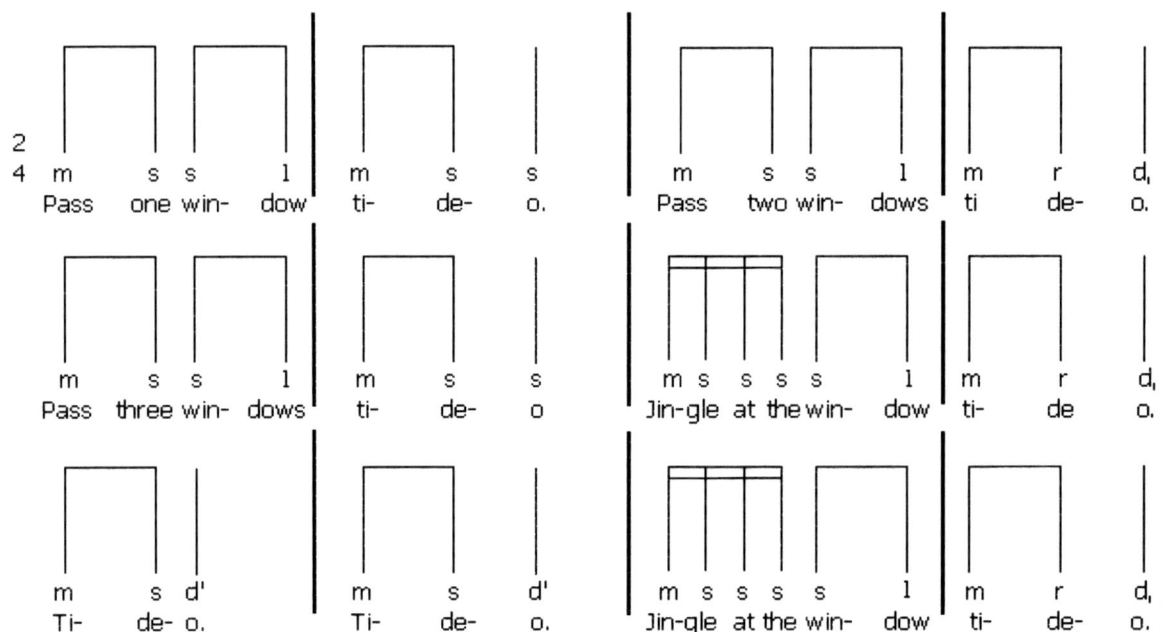

GAME; FORMATION; Circle with arms raised as window. One child skips around the outside of the circle on phrases one and two. On phrase three, he or she circles one of the other children by going through the windows on either side of the chosen child. The child circled joins the first child, and the game is repeated with the two skipping around outside. When the game ends this time the first child joins the circle. No more than two children circling at a time.

LESSON 39 GRADE_____ TEACHER_____

TERMINAL 11 AFTER LESSON 39

BEHAVIORAL OBJECTIVES; students will;
1. Place the measure counts, bar lines and the double bar lines in a rhythm exercise.
2. Write a familiar song on the staff.

MATERIALS; 1. PENCILS AND TERMINAL 11 WORKSHEETS. 2. SCOTLAND'S BURNING WORKSHEETS. 3. OVERHEAD AND WORKSHEET TRANSPARENCIES.

PROCEDURE;
1. GREETING; sung as; Hel- lo   to   you.   (class echoes the same.)
                        d,   s,   s,   d,
                        ta   ti   ti   too-oo

2. OPENING SONG; "Tideo." On this they will;
   a. Sing the words and clap the beat.
   b. Do some form of part work.

SPONGE ACTIVITY;

STATE OBJECTIVES;

3. WORK SHEET ACTIVITY; Teacher leads a short review on writing measure counts. Pencils and terminal 11 worksheets are passed out. Class reads the written directions together and then fills out the worksheets independently.
(BEHAVIORAL OBJECTIVE 1)

4. WRITING ACTIVITY; Presentation song "Scotland's Burning."
   a. "Scotland's Burning" worksheets are distributed.
   b. Class sings the song with words, rhythm, and pitch syllables.
   c. After a brief discussion of the do clef and low so on the leger line, students are to fill in the worksheets independently.
(BEHAVIORAL OBJECTIVE 2)

5. CHANGE OF PACE; Sing several rounds.

6. GOOD-BYE; sung as; Good- bye to   you.   (class echoes the same.)
                        d,   s,   s,   d,
                        ta   ti   ti   too-oo

WRITE ON BOARD; 1. FILL IN A WORKSHEET. 2. WRITE A FAMILIAR SONG ON THE STAFF.

TERMINAL 11   GRADE _____ TEACHER_____

1. Circle the top number of the time signature.
2. Write the measure counts. Place the bar lines and the double bar line.

Write "Scotland's Burning" on the staff.

TERMINAL 11 WORKSHEET NO. TWO OF TWO.

LESSON 40
INSTRUCTIONAL OBJECTIVES;
1. PREPARE the whole note.
2. PRESENT absolute pitch names in G clef.

BEHAVIORAL OBJECTIVES; students will;
1. Learn a new song. (INSTRUCTIONAL OBJECTIVE 1)
2. Learn absolute pitch names for lines and spaces in the G clef.
    (INSTRUCTIONAL OBJECTIVE 2)

MATERIALS; 1. SONG; "RATTLE SNAKE". 2. MAGNETIC BOARD AND PROPERTIES.
3. CHALK BOARDS, CHALK AND ERASERS. 4. FLASH CARDS.

PROCEDURE;
1. GREETING; sung as; Hel-   lo   to   you.   (class echoes the same.)
                         d,   s,   s,   d,
                         ta   ti   ti   too-oo

2. OPENING SONG; "Tideo". On this they will;
    a. Sing the words and clap the beat.
    b. Do some form of part work.

3. FLASH CARD ACTIVITY; Select one or both.

____ a. Known rhythm cards.

____ b. Known solfege / rhythm cards.

STATE OBJECTIVES;

4. NEW SONG; "Rattle Snake". On this they will;
    a. Learn the song by rote.
    b. Clap the beat and sing the words.
    c. Clap the way the words go.
    d. Use inner hearing to internalize the song.
(BEHAVIORAL OBJECTIVE 1)

5. PRESENT G CLEF ABSOLUTE PITCH NAMES; Method of presentation board illustration.
    Distribute chalk boards, chalk and erasers.
    a. Teacher and students draw a G clef on the staff.
    b. Instruction is given for placing notes on a line and then in a space.
    c. Teacher writes a note on each line of the staff. Students do the same.
    d. Teacher tells students that the G clef names the second line G. (Write a G under
        the note on the second line.)
    e. Explain that the music alphabet uses only seven letters of the alphabet to name
        notes. These are used over and over as many times as needed.
    f. Teacher writes the music alphabet; ABCDEFGABCDEFG and lead the students to
        find the names of the other lines from second line G.

133

g. Follow same procedure to name the spaces in G clef.
(BEHAVIORAL OBJECTIVE 2)

6. CLOSURE; 1. Name the song learned today. 2. Name the lines and spaces in G clef.

7. GOOD-BYE; sung as; Good-   bye   to   you.   (class echoes the same.)
                        d,   s,   s,   d,
                        ta   ti   ti   too-oo

WRITE ON BOARD; 1. LEARN A NEW SONG. 2. LEARN NAMES OF LINES AND SPACES IN THE G CLEF.

RATTLESNAKE

LESSON 41
INSTRUCTIONAL OBJECTIVES;
1. PREPARE ti tum.
2. PRESENT (a) High do on the tone ladder. (b) tum ti.
3. PRACTICE absolute pitch names in G clef.

BEHAVIORAL OBJECTIVES; students will;
1. Learn a new song. (INSTRUCTIONAL OBJECTIVE 1)
2. Learn a new pitch syllable. (INSTRUCTIONAL OBJECTIVE 2)
3. Learn a new rhythm sign and it's syllable. (INSTRUCTIONAL OBJECTIVE 3)
4. Review G clef absolute pitch names. (INSTRUCTIONAL OBJECTIVE 4)

MATERIALS; 1. SONG; "CIRCLE ROUND THE ZERO". 2. MAGNETIC DO'. 3. FLASH
CARDS. 4. DOTTED QUARTER NOTE AND EIGHTH NOTE COMBINATION IN THE RHYTHM
DISPLAY AREA. 5. BINDERS.

PROCEDURE;
1. GREETING; sung as; Hel-   lo   to   you.   (class echoes the same.)
                        d,   s,   s,   d,
                        ta   ti   ti   too-oo

2. OPENING SONG; "Rattle Snake." On this they will;
    a. Sing the words and clap the beat.
    b. Do some form of part work.

3. FLASH CARD ACTIVITY; Select one or both.

___ a. Known rhythm cards.

___ b. Known solfege / rhythm cards.

STATE OBJECTIVE;

4. NEW SONG; "Circle Round The Zero". On this they will;
    a. Learn the song by rote.
    b. Clap the beat while singing the words.
    c. Clap the way the words go.
    d. Use inner hearing to internalize the song.
(BEHAVIORAL OBJECTIVE 1)

5. PRESENT HIGH DO ON THE TONE LADDER; Presentation song "Tideo."
    a. Class sings song.
    b. Derives rhythm by singing the rhythm syllables.
    c. Uses the tone ladder and a question mark to derive the melody and find the new
        tone.
    d. Class answers questions about the relationship of the new tone to so. (Is it higher
        or lower? Does it move by a step or a skip?)

e. When the new pitch is identified the name high do is given. The hand sign is shown. The class sings the song again first singing the pitch syllables and then singing the pitch syllables and making the hand signs.
(BEHAVIORAL OBJECTIVE 2)

6. PRESENT TUM TI; Presentation song "Chairs to mend."
    a. Class sings song.
    b. Teacher sings words and claps the beats of the phrase "chairs to."
    c. Class is given time to identify the sign by number of beats and sounds heard.
    d. After the sign is found the syllable tum ti is given. The hand clap is shown and the note types are given.
    e. Class finds song in binder. Claps and sings the rhythm syllables. Then claps the beat and sings the rhythm syllables.
(BEHAVIORAL OBJECTIVE 3)

7. WRITING ACTIVITY; Students will review names of lines and spaces in G clef. Method of presentation;
    a. Teacher will show students how to match letter names with staff positions to spell words.
    b. Students will take turns coming to the board and writing a word on the staff.
(BEHAVIORAL OBJECTIVE 4)

8. CLOSURE; 1. Name the new song learned today. 2. Tell something about the new rhythm sign learned today. 3. Tell something about the new pitch syllable learned today. 4. Name the lines and spaces in G clef.

9. GOOD-BYE; sung as; Good-   bye   to   you   (class echoes the same.)
                         d'   s   s   d'
                         ta   ti   ti   too-oo

WRITE ON BOARD; 1. LEARN A NEW SONG. 2. LEARN A NEW RHYTHM SIGN. 3. LEARN A NEW PITCH SYLLABLE. 4. REVIEW G CLEF LINES AND SPACES.

CIRCLE ROUND THE ZERO

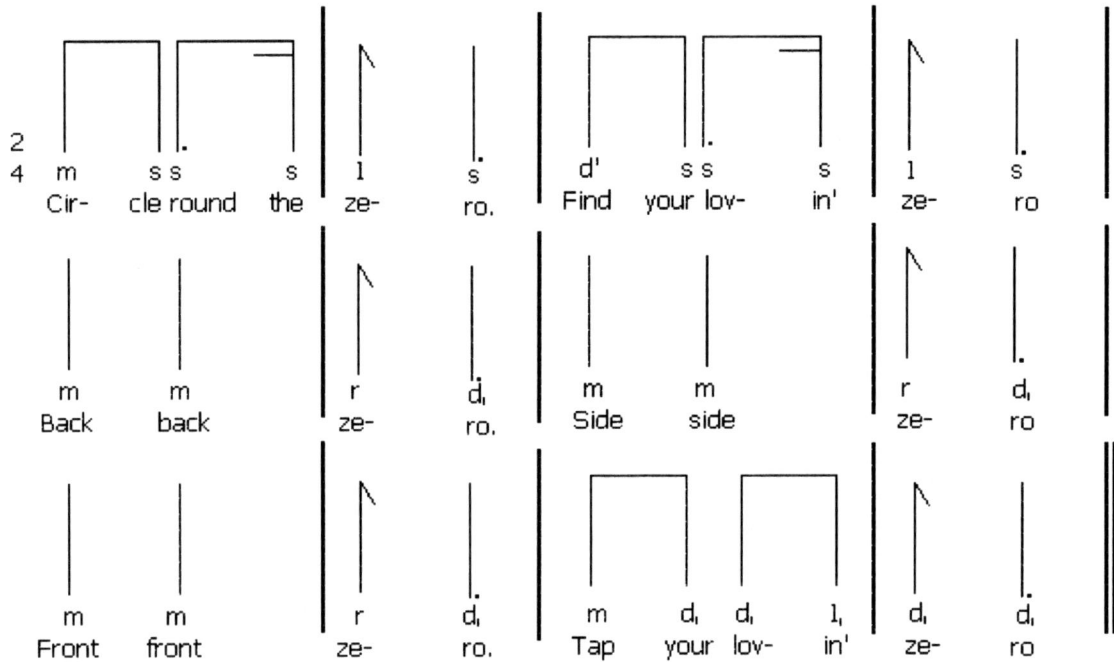

2/4 m	s s	s	l	s	d'	s s	s	l	s
Cir-	cle round	the	ze-	ro.	Find	your lov-	in'	ze-	ro
m	m	r	d,	m	m			r	d,
Back	back	ze-	ro.	Side	side			ze-	ro
m	m	r	d,	m	d, d,	l,	d,	d,	
Front	front	ze-	ro.	Tap	your lov-	in'	ze-	ro	

PLAY PARTY; FORMATION; Double circle with partners facing each other. The inside circle is the zero. The zero circles around the outside circle doing the actions according to the words. On the words "tap your lovin' zero", circles exchange places and the game repeats.

TERMINAL 12 AFTER LESSON 41

BEHAVIORAL OBJECTIVES; students will;
1. Fill in a worksheet for absolute pitch names in G clef.

MATERIALS; 1. PENCILS AND G CLEF WORKSHEETS.

PROCEDURE;
1. GREETING; sung as; Hel-   lo   to   you.   (class echoes the same.)
                        d'   s   s   d'
                        ta   ti   ti   too-oo

2. OPENING SONG; "Circle Round The Zero". On this they will;
   a. Sing the words and clap the rhythm.
   b. Do some form of part work.

SPONGE ACTIVITY;

STATE OBJECTIVES;

3. WRITING ACTIVITY; Pass out pencils and G clef worksheets. Students are to read and
   follow the written directions to fill out the worksheets.
(BEHAVIORAL OBJECTIVE 1)

4. PLAY PARTY; "Tideo". (NEW)

5. GOOD-BYE; sung as; Good-   bye   to   you.   (class echoes the same.)
                      d'   s   s   d
                      ta   ti   ti   too-oo

WRITE ON BOARD; 1. FILL IN A WORKSHEET FOR G CLEF LETTER NAMES.

TERMINAL 12   GRADE _____ TEACHER_____

LESSON 42
INSTRUCTIONAL OBJECTIVES;
1. PRESENT the whole note and the whole rest.
2. PRACTICE absolute pitch names in G clef.

BEHAVIORAL OBJECTIVES;
1. Learn a new song. (INSTRUCTIONAL OBJECTIVE 1)
2. Learn two new rhythm signs. (INSTRUCTIONAL OBJECTIVE 2)
3. Review pitch names in G clef. (INSTRUCTIONAL OBJECTIVE 3)

MATERIALS; 1. SONG; "LIZA JANE". 2. LINES AND SPACES WORKSHEET. 3. PENCILS. 4. FLASH CARDS.

PROCEDURE;
1. GREETING; sung as; Hel-   lo   to   you.   (class echoes the same.)
                                  d'   s   s   d'
                                  ta   ti   ti   too-oo

2. OPENING SONG; "Circle Round The Zero". On this they will;
    a. Sing the words and clap the beat.
    b. Do some form of part work.

3. FLASH CARD ACTIVITY; Select one or both.

___ a. Known rhythm cards.

___ b. Known solfege / rhythm cards.

STATE OBJECTIVES;

4. NEW SONG; "Liza Jane." On this they will;
    a. Learn the song by rote.
    b. Clap the beat and sing the words.
    c. Sing and clap the rhythm syllables.
    d. Use inner hearing to internalize the song.
(BEHAVIORAL OBJECTIVE 1)

5. PRESENT THE WHOLE NOTE; Presentation song "Rattle Snake".
    a. Class sings song.
    b. Teacher sings the last "bite" and claps the beat.
    c. Students are given time to identify the sign by the number of sounds and beats heard.
    d. After identification, the rhythm syllables is given as too-oo-e-oo. The hand clap is shown, and the note type is given.
    e. The whole rest is presented as no sound for four beats. The sign is shown and described.
(BEHAVIORAL OBJECTIVE 2)

PAGE 2 LESSON 42

6. WRITING ACTIVITY; Students will fill in a lines and spaces worksheet. (BEHAVIORAL OBJECTIVE 3)

7. CLOSURE; 1. Name the new song learned today. 2. Tell something about the new rhythm sign learned today.

8. GOOD-BYE; sung as; Good- bye   to   you.   (class echoes the same.)
                          d'   s   s   d'
                          ta   ti   ti   too-oo

WRITE ON BOARD; 1. LEARN A NEW SONG. 2. LEARN TWO NEW RHYTHM SIGNS.
3. REVIEW G CLEF LINES AND SPACES.

LIZA JANE

m	m	r	d	m	s	s	l	s	m	s
Come	my love	and	go	with me,			Lil'	'Li-	za	Jane.
m	m	r	d	m	s	s	m	m	r	d,
Come	my love	and	go	with me,			Lil'	'Li-	za	Jane.
d'	s	l	s	l	s	m	s			
O	E-	li-	za	Lil'	'Li-	za	Jane.			
d'	s	l	s	m	m	r	d,			
O	E-	li-	za	Lil'	'Li-	za	Jane.			

2. I've got a house in Baltimore, Lil' 'Liza Jane.
    Street car runs right by my door. Lil' 'Liza Jane.
    O, Eliza, Lil' 'Liza Jane.
    O, Eliza, Lil' 'Liza Jane.

3. I've got a house in Baltimore. Lil' 'Liza Jane.
    Brussels carpet on the floor. Lil' 'Liza Jane.
    O, Eliza, Lil' 'Liza Jane.
    O, Eliza, Lil' 'Liza Jane.

LESSON 42 GRADE_____ TEACHER_____

140

LESSON 43

INSTRUCTIONAL OBJECTIVES;
1. PREPARE singing phrases.
2. PRESENT (a) High do on the staff. (b) Duration of notes.
3. PRACTICE in tune singing.

BEHAVIORAL OBJECTIVES; students will;
1. Learn a new song. (INSTRUCTIONAL OBJECTIVE 1)
2. Derive a generalization statement for high do. (INSTRUCTIONAL OBJECTIVE 2)
3. Learn about duration of notes. (INSTRUCTIONAL OBJECTIVE 3)
4. Sing familiar songs in solfege. (INSTRUCTIONAL OBJECTIVE 4)

MATERIALS; 1. SONG; "FIRE FLY". 2. SHEET OF PAPER. 3. BINDERS. 4. FLASH CARDS.

PROCEDURE;
1. GREETING; sung as; Hel-   lo   to   you.   (class echoes the same.)
                        d'   s   s   d'
                        ta   ti   ti   too-oo

2. OPENING SONG; "Liza Jane". On this they will;
    a. Sing the words and clap the beat.
    b. Sing as a round.

3. FLASH CARD ACTIVITY; Select one or both.

___ a. Known rhythm cards.

___ b. Known solfege / rhythm cards.

STATE OBJECTIVES;

4. NEW SONG; "Fire Fly". On this they will;
    a. Learn the song by rote.
    b. Clap the beat while singing the words.
    c. Clap and sing the rhythm syllables.
    d. Use inner hearing to internalize the song.
(BEHAVIORAL OBJECTIVE 1)

5. PRESENT HIGH DO ON THE STAFF; Presentation song "Tideo."
    a. Class sings song.
    b. Teacher writes the letters m s d' under the staff.
    c. Tell class we will place so on the second line. Ask class where is mi. (a) First line.
    d. Teacher leads a discussion about d' in relationship to so. Generalization statement
       is derived.
(BEHAVIORAL OBJECTIVE 2)

141

6. PRESENT DURATION OF NOTES. Define duration. Method of presentation — cut a sheet of paper as follows; the whole note is the whole sheet of paper. Then cut the paper in half. This is the half note. Continue until all eight note lengths have been shown and compared.
(BEHAVIORAL OBJECTIVE 3)

7. MUSIC PERFORMANCE. Students will sing familiar songs in solfege.
(BEHAVIORAL OBJECTIVE 4) (Use student binders.)

8. CLOSURE; 1. Name the new song learned today. 2. State the so high do rule.
    3. What is duration?

9. GOOD-BYE; sung as; Good-   bye   to   you   (class echoes the same.)
                          d'   s   s   d'
                          ta   ti   ti   too-oo

WRITE ON BOARD; 1. LEARN A NEW SONG. 2. PLACE HIGH DO ON THE STAFF.
3. LEARN ABOUT DURATION OF NOTES.

FIREFLY

2. Firefly, firefly, may I speak?
    Did you turn your light off are your playing hide and seek?
    Up among the trees I see you peek.

3. Firefly, firefly, please don't go.
    Will you take me with you, I would like to fly you know.
    Up above the trees, I'd love it so.

LESSON 43 GRADE_____ TEACHER_____

TERMINAL 13 AFTER LESSON 43

BEHAVIORAL OBJECTIVES; students will;
1. Identify music signs, symbols and terms on a worksheet.

MATERIALS; 1. PENCILS AND TERMINAL 13 WORKSHEETS.

PROCEDURE;
1. GREETING; sung as;   Hel-   lo   to   you.   (class echoes the same.)
                          d'   s   s   d'
                          ta   ti   ti   too-oo

2. OPENING SONG; "Fire Fly". On this they will;
    a. Sing the words and clap the beat.
    b. Do some form of part work.

SPONGE ACTIVITY;

STATE OBJECTIVES;

3. PITCH ACTIVITY; Sing familiar songs in the binder.

4. WORKSHEET ACTIVITY; Pass out pencils and Terminal 13 worksheets. Students are
    instructed to read and follow the directions and fill out the worksheets.
(BEHAVIORAL OBJECTIVE 1)

5. PLAY PARTIES; Circle Round The Zero. (NEW)

6. GOOD-BYE; sung as; Good- bye   to   you.   (class echoes the same.)
                        d'   s   s   d'
                        ta   ti   ti   too-oo

WRITE ON BOARD; 1. FILL IN A WORKSHEET

TERMINAL 13   GRADE _____ TEACHER_____

143

NAME _____ CLASS _____ DATE _____

Place a letter in front of the symbol or term that describes it.

2

___ 1.

                              A. Lines that are added to the staff.

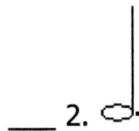

___ 2.

                              B. Dotted half note. One sound for three beats. Spoken as too-oo-e.

3

___ 3.

                              C. The do clef.

___ 4.

                              D. A time signature explained as three beats to a measure and the quarter note gets one beat.

___ 5. Leger lines

                              E. Three sounds for two beats. An eighth note, a quarter note, and an eighth note. Spoken as syn co pa.

4

___ 6.

                              F. A time signature explained as two beats in a measure and a quarter note gets one beat.

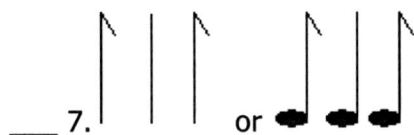

___ 7.   or

                              G. A time signature explained as three beats in a measure and a quarter note gets one beat.

___ 8.

H. A whole note. One sound for four beats. Spoken as too-oo-e-oo.

___ 9. or

I. In music, the length of a sound (a note), or a silence (a rest).

___ 10.

J. A dotted quarter note followed by an eighth note. Two sounds for two beats. Spoken as tum ti.

___ 11. Duration

K. G clef or treble clef. This clef names the second line on the staff G.

___ 12. E, G, B, D, F

L. Letter names of spaces in G clef

___ 13. F, A, C, E

M. Letter names of lines in G clef.

SONGS TO READ

FROM
PREPARE, PRESENT
AND PRACTICE
THE DETAILS OF A
KODALY BASED
PROGRAM

BY
MAXINE BEASLEY

TABLE OF CONTENTS

RAIN RAIN GO AWAY

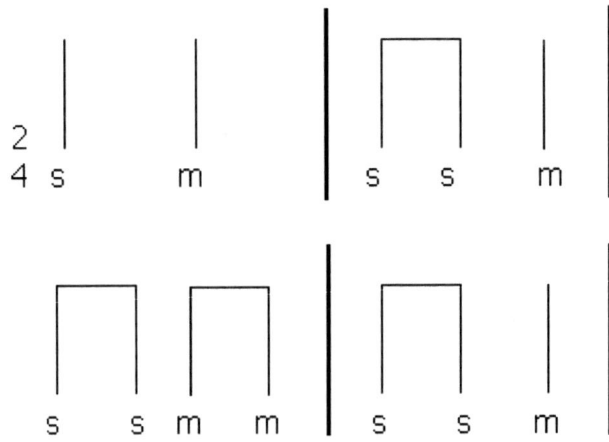

QUAKER, QUAKER

Group 1 (Question)　　　　　　　　　　　　Group 2 (Answer)

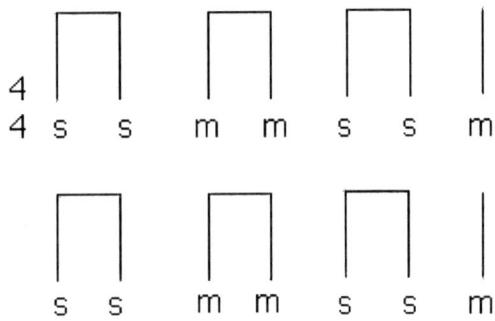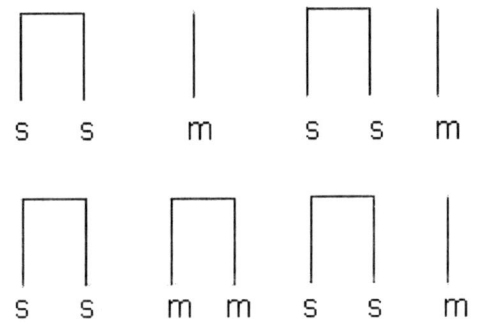

IN AND OUT

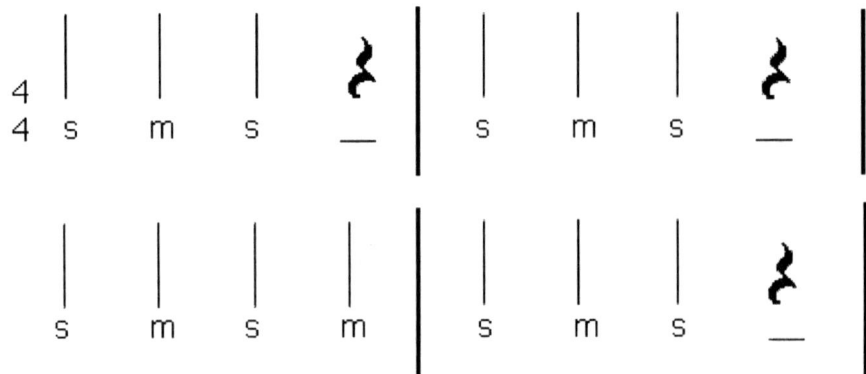

LUCY LOCKETT

2/4 s s l l | s s m m | s s l l | s m |

s s l l | s s m m | s s l l | s m |

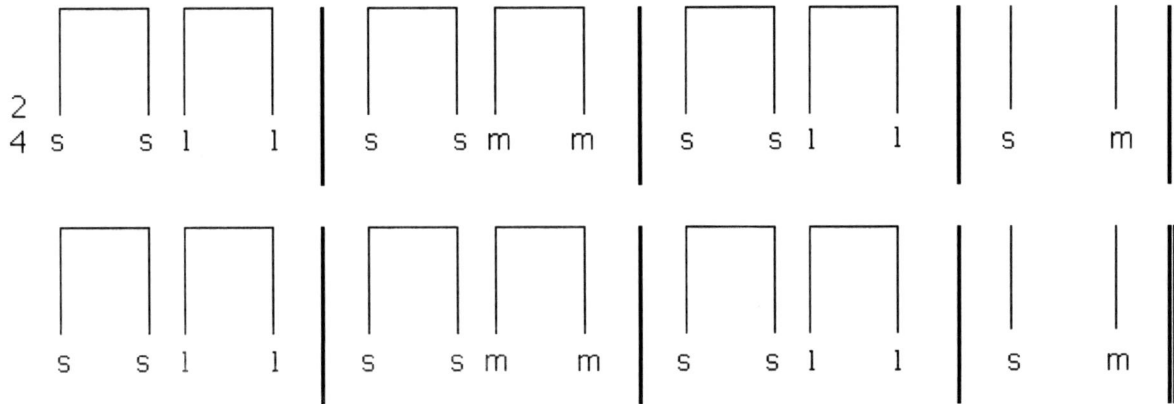

BOUNCE HIGH, BOUNCE LOW

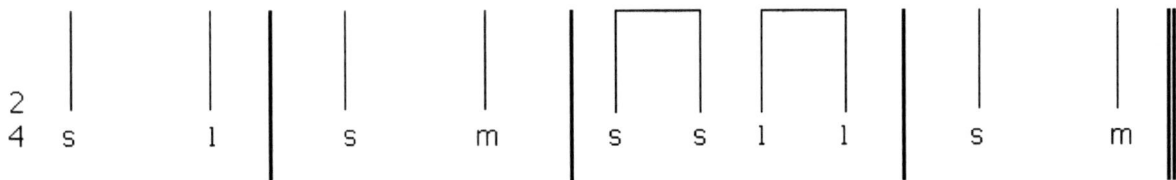

2/4 s l | s m | s s l l | s m ‖

PEAS PORRIDGE HOT

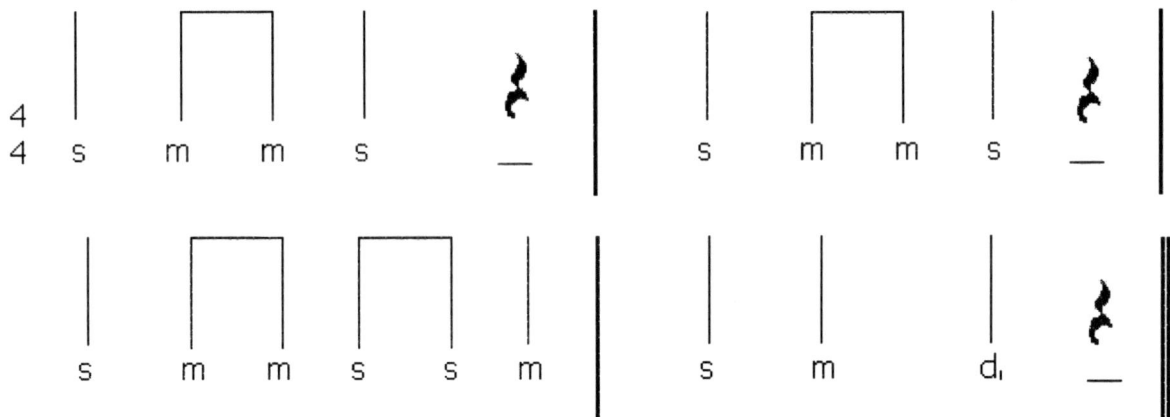

4/4 s m m s 𝄽 | s m m s 𝄽 |

s m m s s m | s m d₁ 𝄽 ‖

150

RING AROUND THE ROSIE

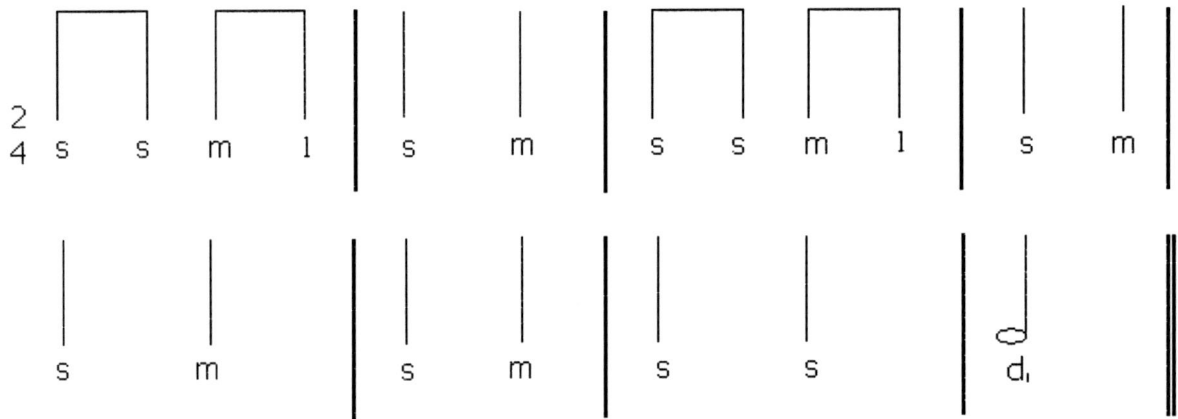

HOT CROSS BUNS

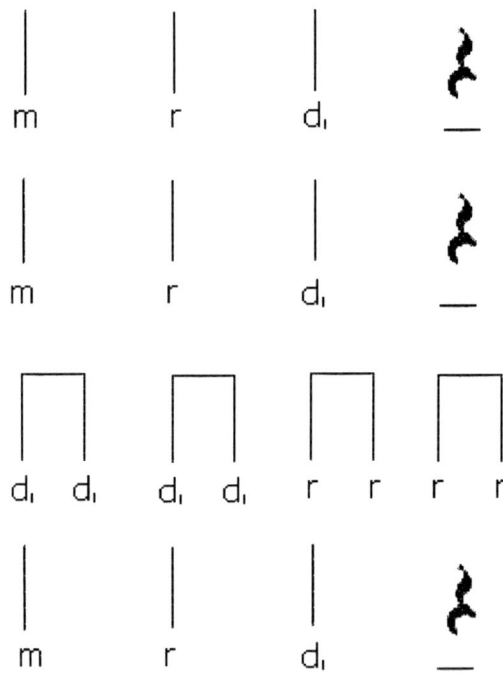

SNAIL, SNAIL

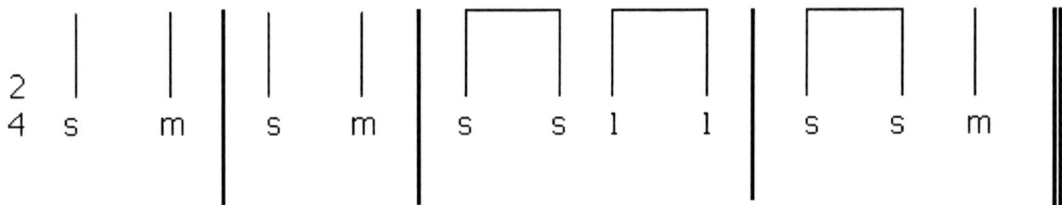

BOW, WOW, WOW

$\frac{4}{4}$ d͵ d͵ d͵ — | m m m m — |

s s s l s m d͵ | m r d͵ — ‖

WHO'S THAT

$\frac{2}{4}$ d͵ | s | r r m m | r d͵ |

d͵ | s | r r m m | d͵ |

d͵ | s | r r m m | r d͵ |

d͵ | s | r r m m | d͵ ‖

HERE COMES A BLUEBIRD

FUZZY WUZZY

TEDDY BEAR

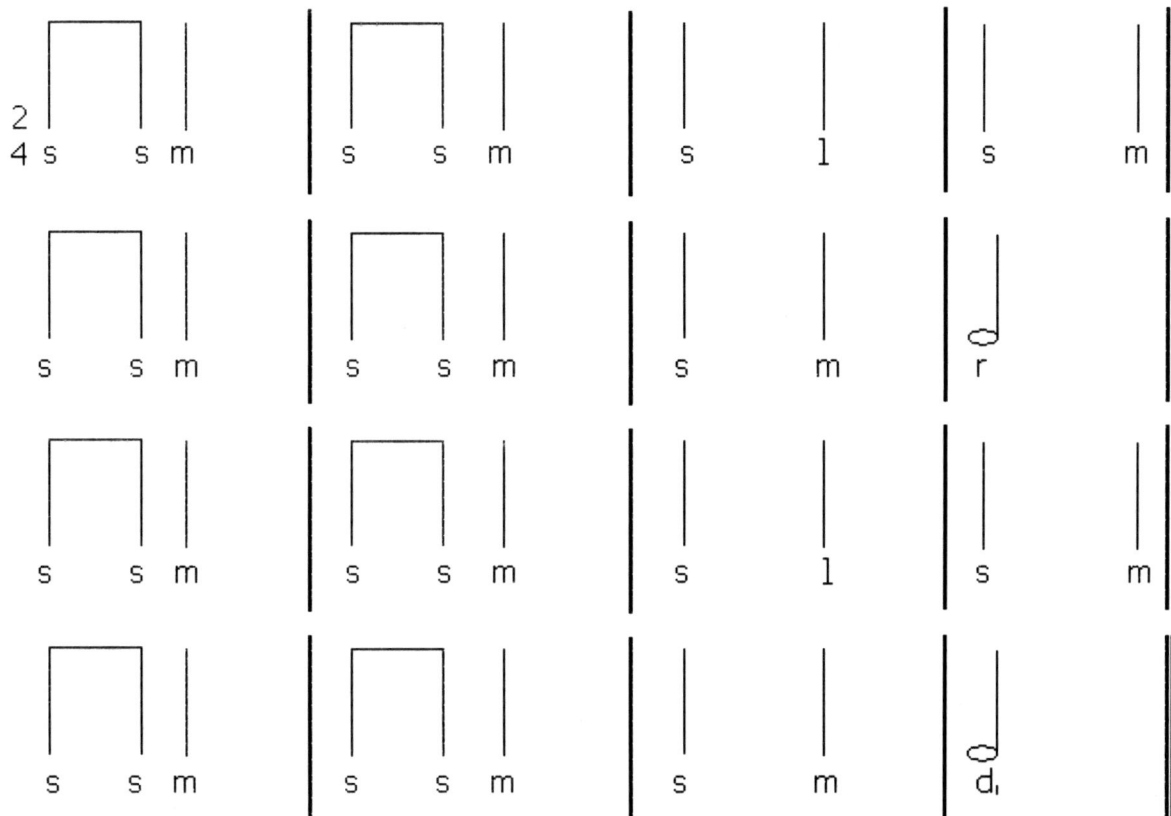

BUTTON YOU MUST WANDER

d, d, d, r | m s | r s | m d, |

d, d, d, r | m s | r s | d, |

l l l | s d, | l l l | s d, |

d, d, d, r | m s | r s | d, ‖

155

DINAH

GREAT GRAND DAD

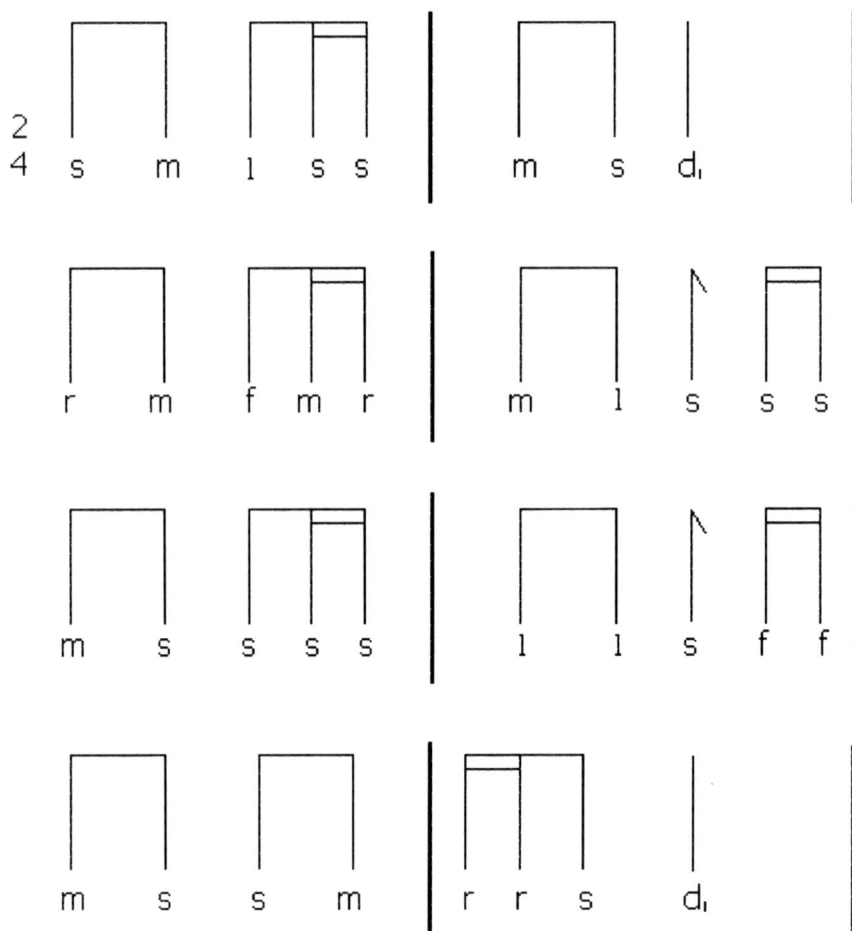

$\frac{2}{4}$ s m | l s s | m s d₁ |

r m | f m r | m l s | s s |

m s | s s s | l l s | f f |

m s | s m | r r s | d₁ ‖

GREAT BIG HOUSE IN NEW ORLEANS

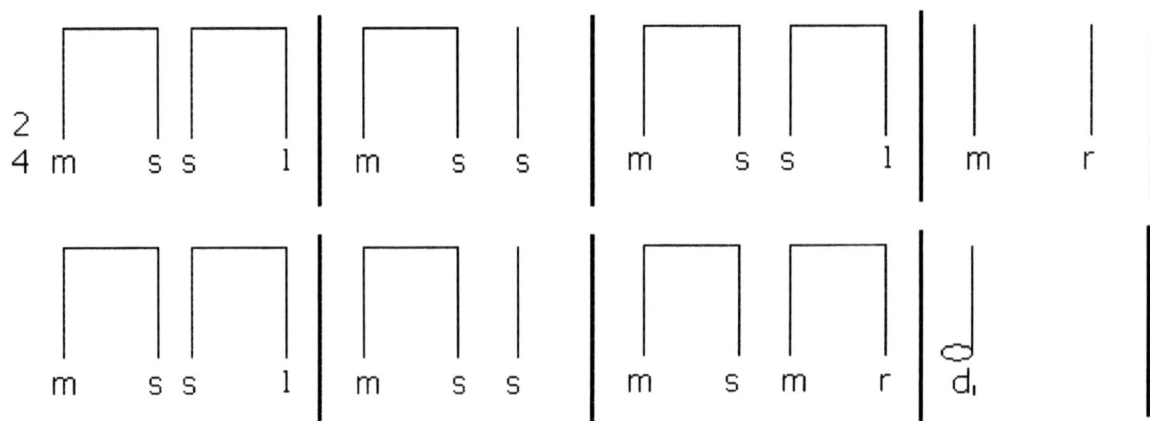

$\frac{2}{4}$ m s s l | m s s | m s s l | m r |

m s s l | m s s | m s m r | d₁ ‖

157

ALABAMA GAL

LET US CHASE THE SQUIRREL

158

DOGGIE, DOGGIE

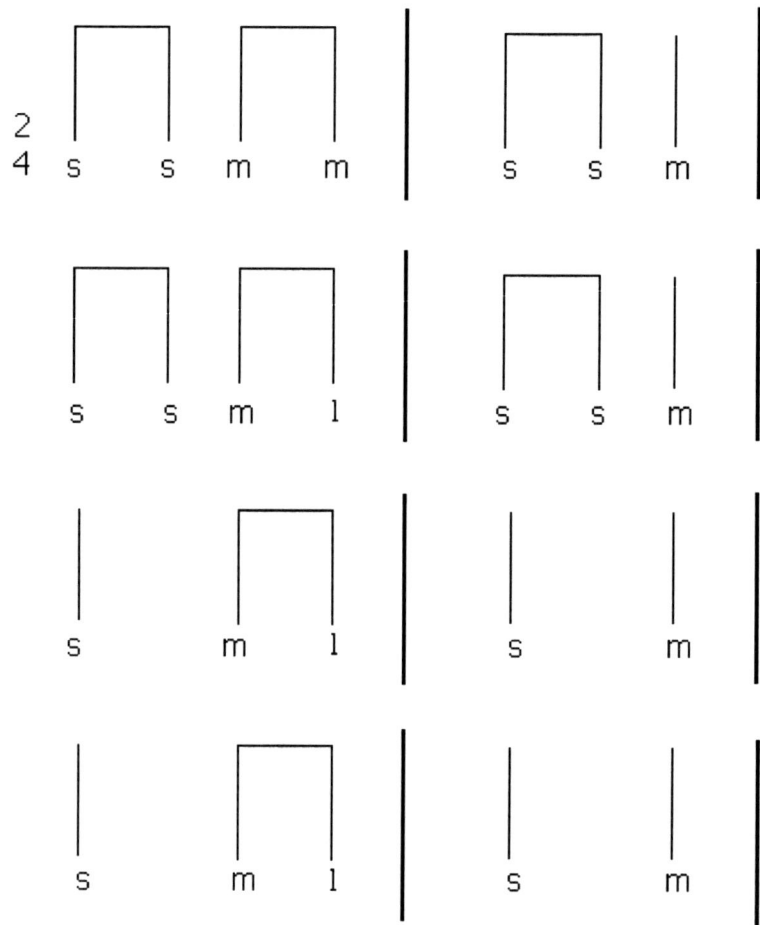

ROCKY MOUNTAIN

2/4 d̩ d̩ d̩ m | d̩ d̩ d̩ m | d̩ d̩ m s | s |

l s m d̩ | l s m d̩ | m m r r | d̩ |

d̩ m | s l | m m r d̩ | r |

d̩ m | s l | m m r r | d̩ ‖

160

WEAVILY WHEAT

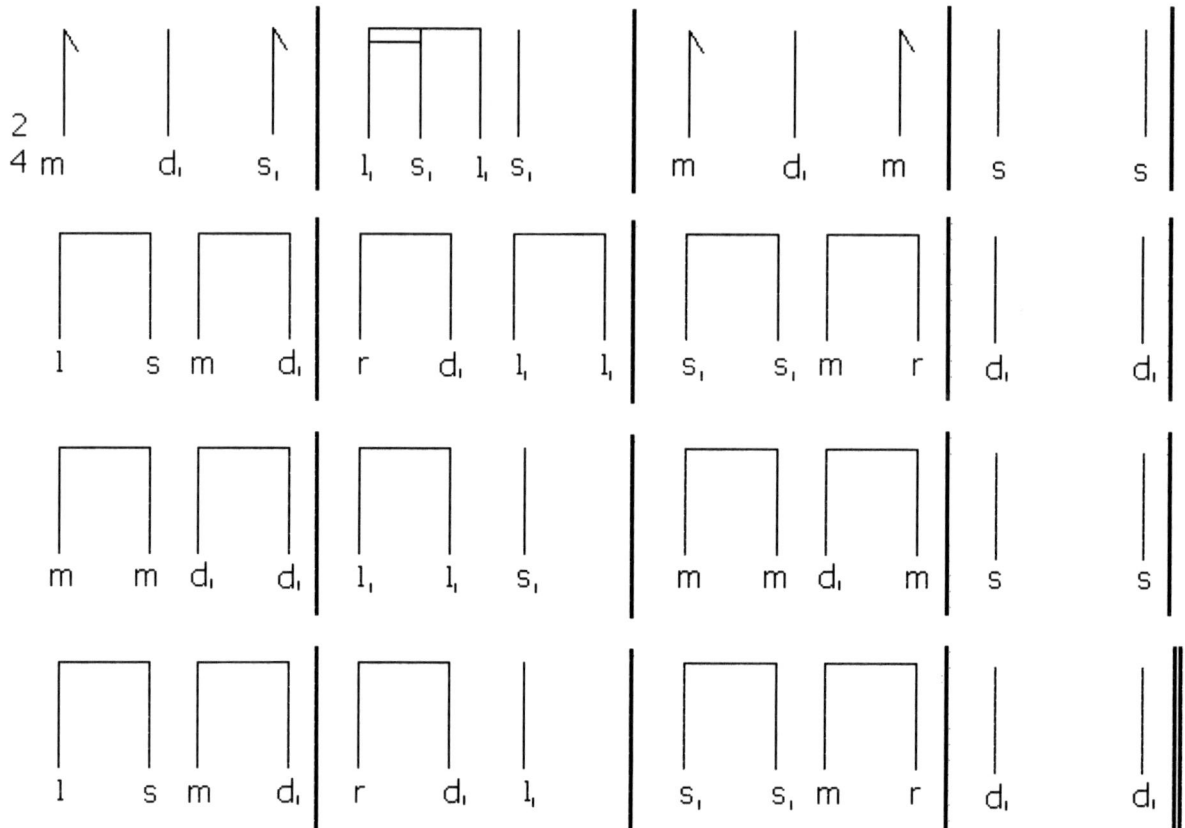

161

KOOKABURRA

$\frac{2}{4}$ s s s s   l l l | s   m   s   m |

m m m m   f f f | m d_1 m d_1 |

d^1 l t d^1 l | s   s l s f |

m d_1 d_1 d_1 | d_1 ‖

SALLY GO ROUND THE SUN

$\frac{2}{4}$ s s s s . l | s   𝄾 | s s s s . l | s   𝄾 |

s s s s . l | s   m | m. m r r | d_1 𝄾 ‖

162

JOHN KANAKA

CHICKAMA, CHICKAMA

$\frac{6}{8}$ d, d, d, d, d, d, | d, l, s, |

d, d, d, d, d, | d, l, s, |

d, d, d, d, d, | d, d, l, s, ||

HUSH LITTLE BABY

$\frac{4}{4}$ s, m m m f | m r r r |

s, s, r r r r m | r d, d, |

s, m m m f | m r r s, |

s, r r m | r d, d, ||

164

RIDING IN A BUGGY

CUMBERLAND GAP

CAMPTOWN LADIES

SCOTLAND'S BURNING

CHAIRS TO MEND

MY GOOD OLD MAN

GLOSSARY

ACCENT. A single tone or chord louder than those around it.

BALLAD. In music, a song that tells a story.

BAND. A balanced group of instruments consisting of woodwinds, brass, and percussion.

BAR LINE. A vertical line that separates music into measures.

BEAT. The repeated pulse that can be felt in some music.

CONTOUR. The shape of a melody.

CONTRAST. Two or more things that are different. In music, slow is a contrast to fast, section A is a contrast to section B.

D. C. AL FINE. Go back to the beginning and stop at fine.

DICTATION. In music a process of writing rhythm, melody or both, as a results of what someone else says.

DO CLEF. A clef sign that locates do on the staff.

DOUBLE BAR LINE. Two vertical lines indicating the end of a selection.

D. S. AL FINE. Go back to the sign and stop at Fine.

DURATION. In music, the length of time a note or rest lasts.

FORM. The overall plan of a piece of music.

G CLEF. A clef sign that names the second line G on the staff.

HARMONY. Two or more different tones sounding at the same time.

LEGER LINES AND SPACES. Added lines above or below the staff.

MEASURE. A grouping of beats set off by bar lines.

MEASURE COUNT. The number of counts in the measure as indicated by the top number of a time signature.

MELODY. A line of single tones that move upward, downward, or repeats.

MUSIC. Organized patterns of sound.

NOTE. A symbol for musical sound.

ORCHESTRA. A balanced group of instruments consisting of strings, woodwinds, brass, and percussion.

OSTINATO. A rhythm or melody patterns that repeats.

PITCH. The highness or lowness of a tone.

REST. A symbol for musical silence.

RHYTHM. In music, the combination of long and short sounds and silences.

ROUND. A follow the leader process in which all sing the same melody but start at different times.

STAFF. A set of five parallel lines on which music notes are written.

STEM. The vertical line attached to a note head. May be used separately for stem notation.

SLUR. A curve line over two or more different notes that are sung on one word.

TEMPO. The speed of the beat in music.

TIE. A curved line connecting two notes on the same pitch. The tie connects the sound of the first note to the second. Therefore making the first note longer.

TONE COLOR. The special sound that makes one instrument or voice sound different from another.

BIOGRAPHY

MAXINE HORTON BEASLEY

Maxine Horton Beasley was born in Marshall, Texas where she attended New Faun Elementary and Pemberton High School. She continued reaching higher educational achievements by receiving a B.S. from Wiley College and a M.A. from Highlands University in Las Vegas, New Mexico and performed Post Graduate work at North Texas State University in Commerce Texas. She received her Kodaly Certification while attending the Festival Institute in Round Top, Texas, which was sponsored by the University of Texas.

Mrs. Beasley's 41 years as a music teacher runs the gamut of all teaching levels from Elementary, Junior High, and High School. From her instruction, students have achieved a high level of recognition through Junior High and High School choirs receiving top level ratings, her High School state choir placed first in contest at Prairie View University and her national male quartet placed first in contest in Atlanta, Georgia. Mrs. Beasley was a level three teacher on the career ladder, the highest level that can be achieved within this teaching evaluation instrument.

Mrs. Beasley found great joy in her teaching and always sought to expand her knowledge about teaching methods that would be helpful to her students. Passing on her teaching experiences in this lesson plan book, she hopes this will be helpful and useful for your teaching experience.

Mrs. Beasley is now retired and serves as pianist and director for all choirs at the St. John Missionary Baptist Church in Beaumont, Texas.

BIBLIOGRAPHY

BEETHOVEN, JANE
WORLD OF MUSIC BOOK 4
Silver Burdett and Ginn
Morristown, New Jersey 1988.

CHOSKY, LOIS AND BRUMMITT, DAVID
120 SINGING GAMES AND DANCES FOR ELEMENTARY SCHOOLS.
Prentice - Hall, Inc.
Englewood Cliffs, New Jersey, 1988.

CHOSKY, LOIS
THE KODALY METHOD
Prentice - Hall, Inc.
Englewood Cliffs, New Jersey, 1981.

DANIEL, KATINKA
KODALY APPROACH METHOD BOOK 2
Mark Foster Music Company.
Champaign, Ill.

ERDEI, PETER
150 AMERICAN FOLK SONGS.
Boosey & Hawkes, Inc. 1988.

LAWRENCE, MARJORIEL
WHAT? ME TEACH MUSIC?
Alfred Publishing company
Sherman Oaks, California 1982.

SEEGER, RUTH CRAWFORD
AMERICAN FOLKSONGS FOR CHILDREN
DoubleDay
Garden City, New York 1948

TRINKA, JILL
FOLKSONGS , SINGING GAMES AND PLAY PARTIES VOL. 1

TACKA, PHILIP AND HOULAHAN, MICHEAL
SOUND THINKING VOLUME 1
Boosey & HawkEs, Inc. 1995

CPSIA information can be obtained at www.ICGtesting.com
Printed in the USA
LVOW09s1847040515

437173LV00005B/264/P